THE COAST GUARD in ACTION

Titles in *U.S. Military Branches and Careers*

The Air Force in Action
ISBN 0-7660-1636-6

The Army in Action
ISBN 0-7660-1635-8

The Coast Guard in Action
ISBN 0-7660-1634-X

The Marine Corps in Action
ISBN 0-7660-1637-4

The Navy in Action
ISBN 0-7660-1633-1

1481

U.S. Military Branches and Careers

THE COAST GUARD in ACTION

Ann Graham Gaines

Elkhart Lake - Glenbeulah

ELEM./MIDDLE SCHOOL LIBRARY

Enslow Publishers, Inc.

40 Industrial Road   PO Box 38
Box 398   Aldershot
Berkeley Heights, NJ 07922   Hants GU12 6BP
USA   UK
http://www.enslow.com

Library of Congress Cataloging-in-Publication Data
Gaines, Ann.
    The Coast Guard in action / Ann Graham Gaines.
       p. cm.— (U.S. military branches and careers)
    Includes bibliographical references (p.) and index.
    ISBN 0-7660-1634-X
    1. United States. Coast Guard—Vocational guidance—Juvenile
literature. [1. United States. Coast Guard—Vocational guidance.
2. Vocational guidance] I. Title II. Series.
VG53 .G35   2001
363.28'6'0973—dc21

                        00-010155

Printed in the United States of America

10 9 8 7 6 5 4 3

To Our Readers: We have done our best to make sure all Internet addresses in
this book were active and appropriate when we went to press. However, the
author and the publisher have no control over and assume no liability for the
material available on those Internet sites or on other Web sites they may link to.
Any comments or suggestions can be sent by e-mail to comments@enslow.com
or to the address on the back cover.

Illustration Credits: All photos are courtesy U.S. Coast Guard, except
for the following: Dover Publications, p. 16; National Archives,
pp. 20–21, 33, 34; *Story of the "Titanic" Cards*, Frank O. Braynard, Dover
Publications, p. 24; U.S. Department of Defense, pp. 44, 54, 84, 109,
110; Corel Corp., p. 87.

Cover Illustration: U.S. Department of Defense (background); U.S.
Coast Guard (inset).

Contents

Extraordinary Lifesavers

Since the 1830s, the United States Coast Guard has staged daring rescues of people lost at sea. Once the Coast Guard was known as the Life-Saving Service. It sent men known as Life-Savers out on patrol every night and whenever a storm came up. In the deep dark howling winds, rain, and sleet of winter storms at sea, they patrolled, walking up and down the nation's shores. Hearing cries for help or spying distress signals, Life-Savers ran to grab lifelines. Or they jumped in surfboats, which they rowed out to sea to rescue people from ships that had gone aground or were sinking off the coast. Today, the ocean continues to pose a very real danger to people and ships. The Coast Guard remains ever on the alert, ready to stage yet another challenging search and rescue. Coast Guard personnel are stationed along the nation's heavily traveled rivers, the Great Lakes, the Atlantic and Pacific Oceans, the Caribbean Sea, and the Gulf of Mexico.

The waters of the Atlantic Ocean off the coast of North Carolina are notoriously dangerous. Summer hurricanes can cause widespread destruction to ships in the area. In the winter, the waters are storm-tossed and cold. Sailors who fall into these waters often die of the cold. The Coast Guard Station at Elizabeth City, North Carolina, whose job it is to aid navigation and rescue lives, stays busy all the time. Guard personnel monitor radio airwaves twenty-four hours a day, seven days a week, listening for distress calls. When they pick up one, they head out to the rescue not only in boats, but in planes and helicopters as well.

On the afternoon of December 5, 1993, the four crewmen of Coast Guard HH-60J Rescue Helicopter 6008 returned from a successful mission to rescue four fishermen from their disabled ship in 18-foot seas and winds that reached nearly 50 miles per hour. It was really nasty weather, and Lieutenant Commander Bruce Jones, the pilot, and the other three crewmen were happy to get home. Even though it was late afternoon, they knew that they would have a short time to find some dry clothes and enjoy a little relaxation. The day's work for these Coast Guardsmen had hardly begun—they consider 100-hour workweeks normal.

Within minutes of their return, the Coast Guard helicopter's crew was alerted to prepare for another rescue. More than 170 miles east, the 52-foot sailboat

Duchess was sinking in the storm. The mast had broken under an especially large wave and fallen across the hull of the ship. The sails and the rigging lying on the deck made conditions especially dangerous for the crew. As the wave-tossed *Duchess* began to take on water, the three crewmen radioed their position to the Coast Guard. Their message also said they were preparing to abandon ship.

The Coast Guard knew that if the men panicked and jumped overboard, they would probably be lost. The Guardsmen had to get there as soon as possible. With a Hercules HC-130H turboprop as an escort, Commander Bruce Jones and his crew arrived at the *Duchess*'s last known position just as the sun was setting to the west. The turboprop circled the area at a high altitude, keeping constant radio contact with the helicopter and the shore. The radio equipment aboard the *Duchess* had stopped working and visibility was terrible. It was quickly getting dark, the wind was gusting to over 70 miles per hour, and the tops of the 25-foot waves were being whipped into a fine white stinging spray that made everything else invisible.

As darkness fell, the warning light on the instrument panel signaled that one of the helicopter's engines had caught fire. Commander Bruce turned the helicopter toward land and began emergency procedures. Suddenly, the fire warning light went out and a visual inspection of the engine revealed no problems. At the same time, the helicopter crew spotted the mast light of the *Duchess* in the darkness ahead. Despite a

Helicopters must always be ready for rescue missions. They may be called at any time, day or night, just as the crew aboard the HC-130H turbo was in the case of the sinking *Duchess*.

potential emergency aboard, the helicopter made for the stricken boat. The crew of the *Duchess* heard or saw the helicopter and fired a flare to pinpoint their location. The helicopter was soon directly over the *Duchess*. Its sails were in tatters and the rigging of the ship had fallen onto the battered hull. The *Duchess* was sinking fast. Confident that the helicopter rescue team would be able to save them, the three crew members of the *Duchess* jumped overboard. However, it was not as simple as they thought. The men were quickly swallowed up in the darkness. Finding them again would be a problem.

To make matters worse, once again the fire-warning light went off aboard the helicopter. Another visual inspection revealed no problem, so Commander Bruce continued with the rescue. From 30 feet above the water, the helicopter lowered Guardsman Scott Adlon into the water with a safety harness. During the entire rescue, Commander Bruce kept the helicopter poised barely above the tops of the monstrous waves crashing below. The helicopter crew was busy keeping the line taut as Adlon searched for the sailors in the frigid waters. As he found each sailor, the sailor was put into the safety harness and hauled aboard the helicopter. It was a tough but successful rescue. For the crew of helicopter 6008, it was the last mission that night.

What they did was not special for the United States Coast Guard. The Coast Guard continues to save lives at a steady pace. Records over a one-year period show that the people of the Coast Guard save an average of fourteen lives every day.

In 1994 Commander Bruce and the crew of helicopter 6008 were honored as the winners of the Igor I. Sikorsky Award for Humanitarian Service. Scott Adlon was singled out for the special heroism he displayed during the rescue of the three shipwrecked crewmen.[1]

In both small and large disasters, the Coast Guard is usually the first on the scene. In 1986 when the space shuttle *Challenger* exploded during launch and fell into the ocean, it was Coast Guard boats that raced to search the wreckage. Similarly, in the summer of 1999, when the small plane piloted by John Fitzgerald Kennedy, Jr., was reported late touching down on its flight from Fairfield, New Jersey, to Martha's Vineyard, Massachusetts, it was the First Coast Guard District and Air Force Rescue Coordination Center that launched the initial search. Again that fall, Coast Guard ships and planes were the first to search for an EgyptAir jet when Flight 990 went down in the ocean with hundreds of passengers aboard. These disasters had no survivors. The Coast Guard's job became one of picking up the debris from the surface of the water and from the ocean floor so that investigators could try to determine what caused these crashes, and, perhaps, prevent similar ones in the future.

Although the Coast Guard is usually noted in the newspapers and on television for the daring rescues it performs, the majority of Coast Guard personnel today are involved in tasks that have little to do with search and rescue. When the Coast Guard was first formed, it was called the Revenue Service, and its only job was to collect import duties and to stop smugglers. Saving lives, maintaining lighthouses and harbor buoys, watching out for icebergs, stopping illegal immigrants and drugs from reaching our shores, and acting as a partner to the navy during wartime situations were all jobs that were added later. Today, the Coast Guard performs all of its responsibilities around the world with dedication and courage. The history of the Coast Guard is a story of heroism and duty well performed.

The men and women in the U.S. Coast Guard risk their lives every day saving others. The helicopters they fly and the ships they sail help them keep the waters safe.

History of the Coast Guard

Just after the signing of the Declaration of Independence, what had been the thirteen British colonies in North America formed an agreement to share the same central government—a union that called itself the United States of America. At first, a document called the Articles of Confederation spelled out how this government was to work.

Under the Articles of Confederation, state governments held almost all the powers. States issued their own money, ran their own post offices, and collected their own taxes. The government of the United States was not allowed to collect taxes for itself but depended on handouts from the states to run its programs and to pay its employees. American leaders like George Washington soon came to accept the need for a stronger central government with the power to pay itself. A Constitutional Convention was called, and the delegates from each of the states drew up a new plan of government. One of the first things the new Congress did was to pass a law that taxed goods brought into the country. These taxes were payable to the federal government. As a result, the fate of the federal government no longer depended on the various states. One of the next things the Congress did, guided by Secretary of the Treasury Alexander Hamilton, was create a police force to enforce its new tax laws.

The Revenue Service (1789–1915)

On August 4, 1789, President Washington signed into law the ninth act of the new Congress designed to fight smuggling. The Revenue Service—also called the Revenue Marine Service and the Revenue Cutter Service—was created to enforce the new tax laws. It was authorized to collect the taxes owed to the government by the regular legal merchant vessels and to stop and seize boats it found smuggling along the thousands of miles of coast stretching from Massachusetts to Georgia.

A year later, on August 4, 1790, Congress appropriated the Revenue Service enough money to build ten ships that would make it possible to inspect ships using the nation's waters. The Revenue Bill also provided salaries for one hundred men and arms for the ships. Each ship had a crew of ten men and a monthly payroll of $120.

Alexander Hamilton

When George Washington appointed Alexander Hamilton as the first Secretary of the Treasury in 1789, the nation drastically needed money. This was partly because it had just gone into

debt, having promised to pay back monies states had borrowed to fight the Revolution. In the days before an income tax, the money from import duties was very important. As a young man in the West Indies watching the rum smugglers depart for the American coastline, Alexander Hamilton learned how to avoid paying import duties. As the first Secretary of the Treasury of the newly created United States of America, he was given the responsibility to beat the smugglers at their own game. He supervised the creation of the Revenue Service, which became the Coast Guard in 1915.

Alexander Hamilton lobbied Congress to agree to give Revenue Service officers military rank, just like their navy counterparts. The first commissioned officer in the new service was Hopley Yeaton. In 1799, the government authorized a Revenue Cutter Service Ensign, or flag, which featured sixteen perpendicular stripes, alternating red and white, with the arms of the United States in dark blue on a white field. The sixteen stripes stood for the number of states in the United States at the time.

All of the American states had coastlines along the Atlantic Ocean. Almost all merchant business was conducted by sea. American whalers and cargo ships sailed to all of the world's oceans and brought back both luxuries and the raw materials for commerce. Merchant ships from European countries arrived with their cargo holds full of manufactured goods and returned to their home ports with timber, whale oil, and produce from the United States. All of these cargoes were supposed to pay a small tax to the new central government. Most of the merchants paid these taxes regularly, but there was a core group of merchants who never paid these taxes.

A large amount of the goods arriving in the United States were not carried on large cargo ships or did not pass through an official port of entry. Instead they landed in unlit remote bays and rivers throughout the states. Landing illegal goods or landing goods without paying their duties, or lawful taxes, is called smuggling. Since the earliest colonies were formed, smuggling was widely practiced all along the coastline of the United States. Early colonial industries, such as distilling rum using the sugar from the islands of the West Indies, financed a large and worldwide American merchant navy.[1] Many merchants resented having the government, any government, collect taxes on their goods. George Washington's appointee to head the Revenue Service, Alexander Hamilton, had grown up in the Caribbean, where he saw rumrunners depart on their weekly journeys to the Florida and Georgia coasts. He knew how smugglers operated. He was the perfect man to direct the efforts to capture them.[2]

The Revenue Service was created to prevent contraband (illegal goods) from entering the United States. Today, the Revenue Service no longer exists. The Coast Guard has taken its place. Small craft, like the fast Coastal Interceptor, carry their crews on rescue and law enforcement missions.

Revenue Service cutters regularly ranged beyond the territorial waters of the United States. Captains of American ships often reported observing pirate ships in the waters near the West Indies. Revenue Service cutters were the perfect size to chase the pirates up their shallow water hideaways along the coasts of Cuba and Jamaica. Revenue Service cannons were usually enough to make the pirates give up, but sometimes it took a boarding and swift swordplay to stop the pirates. As the Midwestern United States opened to trade and settlement, American ships began to venture up and down the nation's navigable rivers and into the Great Lakes. Soon the Revenue Service assumed responsibility for protecting American vessels on those lakes and the Mississippi River.

Revenue cutters also began to enforce navigation laws. They ventured out onto the high seas to enforce laws against plundering. After the slave trade was outlawed between the United States and several other countries in 1794, they searched for the huge ships that illegally carried hundreds of Africans chained below decks. As late as 1846, the annual report of the Revenue Service stated that during that year several slave ships had been captured in the Florida Keys. Such captures seem to have been typical.[3]

In July 1797, with the possibility of war with France looming, Congress expanded the Revenue Service agency's responsibilities to include working with the navy to guard the nation's harbors and even to protect American shipping at sea. Revenue cutters helped the navy protect American ships from French and English vessels that routinely stopped ships at sea and kidnapped their sailors.

Several times during the nineteenth century, Revenue cutters again assumed a military role. During the War of 1812, Revenue Service cutters fought alongside navy ships. Revenue crews supported the navy, too, in the Seminole Wars in Florida. Revenue cutters went to the Gulf of Mexico to help blockade the Mexican coast during the Mexican War, which lasted from 1846 to 1848. During the Civil War,

Revenue Service vessels formed most of the Union blockade of the coastline of the Confederate states. One such Revenue Service blockader, the *Harriet Lane*, became the first vessel to fire a shot in the war when it opened fire on the Confederate *Nashville* at Fort Sumter. The ship was present for the surrender of Galveston, but was later captured by Confederates, who used it as a blockade-runner. After the Civil War, the Revenue Service returned to its normal duties.

As the nineteenth century came to a close, Revenue Service cutters joined navy ships in a blockade of Cuba during the Spanish-American War. As the United States expanded, so did the Revenue Service. Hawaii was annexed to the United States in 1898, and it was not long before a Revenue Service cutter was stationed there. In 1909, the Revenue cutter *Thetis* was homeported in Hawaii

The interior of Fort Sumter, in Charleston Harbor, at the beginning of the Civil War. The *Harriet Lane*, a Revenue Service blockader, was the first vessel to fire a shot in the war, when it fired across the bow of the Confederate *Nashville*.

and began a seven-year career as the voice of the American government in the Pacific Ocean region, from the Hawaiian Islands to the Aleutian Islands and the coast of Alaska.[4]

Captain John Faunce

John Faunce was the captain of the Revenue Service side-wheel cutter *Harriet Lane* in 1857. Captain Faunce took the new ship to South America as a part of a navy project to explore the Paraguay and Parana rivers. After their return in 1859, Captain Faunce patrolled the waters off the coast of Florida to prevent renegade slave ships from landing. At the very beginning of the Civil War, Captain Faunce was sent to deliver supplies to Fort Sumter, under bombardment in Charleston Harbor, but the relief mission arrived too late. Fort Sumter had surrendered. Captain Faunce ordered that a shot be fired across the bow of the steamer *Nashville* to force the ship to identify itself. It was the first shot fired from any naval vessel in the long Civil War.

In 1915, Congress passed a law joining two government agencies, the Life-Saving Service and the Revenue Service, to form the Coast Guard Service. The Life-Saving Service, based on land, had thus far been performing rescues from the country's beaches, while the Revenue Service had been operating on the sea and along the coasts from its start. (The Life-Saving Service is presented later in this chapter.)

After the United States entered World War I, the entire Coast Guard was temporarily transferred from the authority of the Treasury Department to the Navy Department. Although the Coast Guard organization stayed in place, some five thousand

Coast Guardsmen sailed aboard navy ships. In fact, members of the Coast Guard commanded some navy ships. Fifteen Coast Guard cutters also took part in the war. During Prohibition, Coast Guard vessels played an important role in preventing ships from smuggling alcohol into the country.

From the beginning of their service, Revenue cutters had come to the aid of ships in distress whenever the cutters happened upon them. In 1831, however, rescue became a regular responsibility of the Revenue cutters. In that year the Revenue Service dedicated some of its men to search out ships and men in distress. When the weather turned cold each year, the Revenue Service began winter cruising, sending seven cutters with rescue equipment to patrol places where sailing ships were often known to founder in bad weather. It was a decision that saved many lives. The Revenue Service could now find the ships in need before a disaster happened. They were sooner on the scene of wrecks and sinkings. Every moment saved more lives.[5]

Icebreaking

In 1867, the United States bought the huge territory of Alaska from Russia. American whaling fleets soon began hunting all over the Pacific Ocean, from the icy waters off the coast of Antarctica to the Arctic Ocean in the north. Every year, American whalers and fishermen fell overboard, got stranded on the winter ice, or were wrecked and stranded along the rocky shores.

In 1871, thirty-three whaling ships were caught in the ice in the Bering Sea. The Revenue Service saved all of the crewmen, but the ice crushed the ships. In 1880, the Revenue Service began to regularly patrol the icy waters of the Pacific Ocean near the north-western coast of Alaska in the cutter *Corwin*. In 1886, the cutter *Bear* replaced the *Corwin* and began a distinguished career of

This painting by the artist Willy Stoewer depicts the sinking of the *Titanic* in the North Atlantic in 1912. After this tragedy, the Coast Guard began watching and reporting on the icebergs that broke off the glaciers of Greenland each year.

service that included icebreaking and lifesaving. After the sinking of the *Titanic*, the Coast Guard was assigned another duty in the North Atlantic Ocean— that of watching and reporting on the roughly seven thousand icebergs that break off the west Greenland glaciers each year.

During World War II, the Coast Guard continued ice patrols as a part of its regular cruises in the North Atlantic. In 1965, by an agreement between the Department of the Treasury and the Department of Defense, the Coast Guard assumed all of the responsibility for icebreaking operations for the military. Today, icebreakers clear a channel through hundreds of miles of heavy ice by slowly running their massive reinforced bottoms onto the ice. This is done repeatedly until the icebreaker finally breaks through the ice. The process is long, tedious, and extremely hazardous. Icebreakers have sometimes gotten caught in the ice and had to wait for spring thaw to break free.

The Life-Saving Service (1789–1915)

As early as 1787, settlers living along the coast in the state of Massachusetts established a volunteer effort to rescue and aid the shipwrecked. Eventually, there were primitive lifesaving stations with life jackets and other lifesaving gear like ropes and pulleys stored in several stations in the various states along the Atlantic coast. Sometimes there were lifeboats, but too often they were not seaworthy or they were missing altogether. For years there were too few lifesaving stations, too few people to maintain them, and little or no money available for equipment.

In 1848, Congressman William Newell of New Jersey, with the support of a former president, John Quincy Adams, succeeded in adding an amendment to a lighthouse bill, appropriating $10,000 to establish eight boathouses, or lifesaving stations, on the northern New Jersey coast from Sandy Hook to Little Egg

Harbor. About every 10 miles, simple 1½-story boathouses measuring 16 by 28 feet were constructed, containing surfboats, rockets, and guns for protecting life and property along the coast. By the fall of 1849, these unmanned facilities were operational, and Congress immediately approved $20,000 more to expand the Life-Saving Service. Eight boathouses were built along the Long Island coast, and six more were

Icebreaker ships run their heavy, reinforced bottoms onto the ice until it breaks. In this way they create channels in the ice, making the waters safer for smaller craft.

built in New Jersey. In the early 1850s, boathouses were located from Rhode Island to North and South Carolina, Georgia, Florida, and Texas. By 1854 lifesaving stations also provided service on the Great Lakes. In 1853 the station keepers were paid a wage for the first time, though it was not enough.

In 1854 many sailors died in a single terrifying storm. Congress responded to this tragedy by establishing more stations, and providing funds to be used for one full-time station keeper for each station. But even this remained too little. Each station keeper had to find volunteers every time a ship was in peril. The station keeper had to walk for miles to notify volunteers they were needed.

During the Civil War, the Life-Saving Service was ignored. In 1870, however, many sailors died in another vicious storm. Newspapers ran articles exposing the sorry state of the nation's lifesaving stations. In 1871 the

Sumner Kimball

In February 1871, Sumner Kimball was appointed chief of the Revenue Marine Bureau. Through Kimball's able administration, the Life-Saving Service quickly took on the characteristics of an efficient and effective organization. The new chief personally inspected the stations in the most dangerous districts, replaced incapable officers with more suitable men, and constructed new lifesaving stations. He was the only person to serve as the Superintendent of the Life-Saving Service until his retirement in 1915. At that time, the Life-Saving Service had expanded to include 285 stations around the country.

Revenue Marine Bureau got a new chief, Sumner Kimball. He sent Captain John Faunce on an inspection tour of the stations. Faunce's report described boathouses with aged keepers and rusting equipment. With this information, Kimball went to Congress to ask for $200,000 to fix the problems. He got new stations and enough personnel to staff each station with six men. The crews followed routines and were occupied drilling, cleaning and fixing equipment, and performing lookout duty.

Of course, during emergency rescues everything changed. During storms and at night, beach patrols walked up and down the beaches, armed with flares. Surf men patrolled the beaches even on nights when they were covered with ice and bitter winds blew. Lifesaving had become a profession. By 1875, there were new stations from Florida to Maine and along the Great Lakes.

Second Lieutenant Ellsworth P. Bertholf

On December 16, 1897, Second Lieutenant E. P. Bertholf and two others were put ashore in the middle of an ice storm on Nelson Island, near Cape Vancouver. Their mission was to travel overland through the midwinter dark and cold to above the Arctic Circle to deliver emergency supplies to over a hundred whalers who were stranded on Point Barrow. These three men drove more than 440 reindeer in temperatures below minus 30 degrees Fahrenheit. Bertholf and the others organized the refugee whalers and delivered medical care. The United States Congress awarded special gold medals for their heroic service.

ELKHART LAKE I M O

These lifesaving stations were well constructed and fully equipped for the many tasks needed to rescue those in distress in the waters off the Atlantic coast. Each station had four rooms on the first floor, two on the second floor, and an observation area above that. The station lifeboat was 26 feet long and seven feet wide, and it weighed between 700 and 1,100 pounds. Lifeboats carried a crew of seven, a commander and six rowers. Their ability to save lives was legendary.[6]

Later, stations would open on the Gulf of Mexico and the Pacific Ocean. In 1878, the U.S. Life-Saving Service became a separate government agency. Kimball became its superintendent. He retired in 1915, when the U.S. Coast Guard was established. By that time, his service had gained fame. The public called lifesavers "soldiers of the surf" and "storm warriors."[7] But their job was changing. Steam engines had first been used to power a ship in 1819. Clipper ships still raced across the oceans in the 1880s, but sailing ships were becoming fewer and fewer.[8] Once steam engines began to power ships, there were fewer ships driven ashore by storms. On the other hand, lifesavers began to be called on to rescue people from small, gas-powered pleasure boats.

By the time the Life-Saving Service merged with the Revenue Service in 1915 to form the U.S. Coast Guard, there was a network of over 270 stations covering the Atlantic, Pacific, and Gulf Coasts and along the Great Lakes. Between 1874 and 1915, the

Service had come to the aid of 28,121 vessels and 178,741 people.[9] The heroic men and women of the Life-Saving Service had saved the equivalent of the population of a small city. These selfless public servants created a proud heritage, and it was with pride that the Life-Saving Service merged with the Revenue Service to create the United States Coast Guard.

The U.S. Lighthouse Service

The first lighthouse in the American colonies was built in Boston in 1716. Before then, colonists lit bonfires or set barrels of pitch on fire in order to guide ships into port at night. The Lighthouse Service was founded in 1789. It took over and built lighthouses, then staffed them with lighthouse keepers. Some lighthouses marked busy port entrances. Others were built on lonely stretches of land near dangerous shoals. Many keepers had

Admiral Russell Randolph Waesche

Russell Randolph Waesche (pronounced "way-she") graduated from the Revenue Cutter Service School in Arundel Cove, Maryland, in 1906. He battled rumrunners off the coast of Connecticut as the captain of the destroyer *Beale* (DD-40). He was promoted over many of his senior officers by President Franklin Roosevelt to become the Commandant of the Coast Guard in 1936. He became the Coast Guard's first vice-admiral in 1942 and its first admiral in 1943. Under his direction, the Coast Guard was used for convoy and amphibious landings as a part of the U.S. Navy. Two of his sons served in the Coast Guard during World War II.

families who helped maintain lighthouses and sea markers and who kept signal lights lit to help ships' captains identify where they were. Lighthouse keepers and their helpers also rescued people from ships that went down near their stations. They rescued people in their lifeboats, and they took in and cared for sailors washed up on shore.

In 1820, the Lighthouse Service staged a successful experiment, establishing the nation's first Lightship Station. This was a small, moored boat that had been decked over to protect its signal light. After 1852, Lighthouse Service personnel not only manned and maintained lighthouses, but also produced navigational aids, drawing up maps and charts and writing books and pamphlets for commercial mariners. Congress made the Lighthouse Service part of the Coast Guard in 1939.

World War II

During World War II, the entire Coast Guard was again transferred to the authority of the Navy Department. Over 171,000 Coast Guardsmen served in that war. They manned 802 Coast Guard vessels as well as 351 navy ships and 288 army ships. Some patrolled the coasts of the United States. Here in the United States, Coast Guardsmen participated in the capture of a team of German saboteurs on a beach in Long Island, New York. Thousands of Guardsmen served in Europe and in the Pacific. Their responsibilities included securing harbors, operating

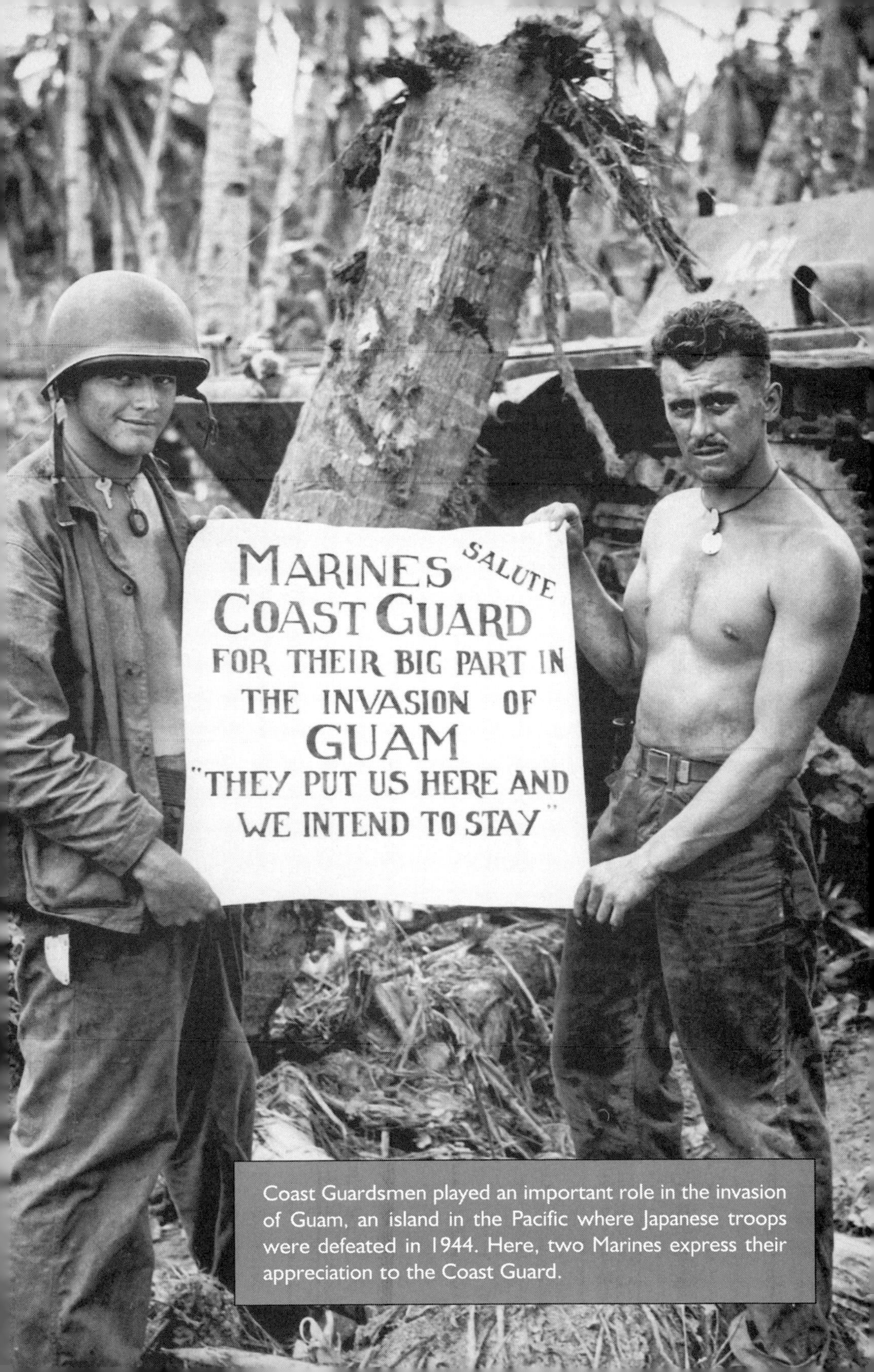
MARINES SALUTE
COAST GUARD
FOR THEIR BIG PART IN
THE INVASION OF
GUAM
"THEY PUT US HERE AND
WE INTEND TO STAY"

Coast Guardsmen played an important role in the invasion of Guam, an island in the Pacific where Japanese troops were defeated in 1944. Here, two Marines express their appreciation to the Coast Guard.

Here, Coast Guardsmen on the deck of the U.S. Coast Guard cutter *Spencer* watch the explosion of a depth charge, which defeated a German U-boat's efforts to break into the center of a large convoy.

landing craft, rescuing soldiers and marines from the surf during landings, and manning escort ships. All together, Guardsmen served on close to fifteen hundred ships.

The Congressional Medal of Honor was awarded posthumously to Signalman First Class Douglas C. Munro, who rescued a detachment of marines trapped by the Japanese on Guadalcanal. Munro died when, to cover the evacuation of the marines, he put his landing craft between the Japanese and the marines.

While patrolling the coast of Greenland, the ice-breaker *Northland* became the first American ship of the war to capture an enemy vessel when it seized the German *Buskoe*. Another Coast Guard vessel, *Icarus*, while out on an anti-submarine patrol, used depth charges to force a Nazi sub to the surface. There, faced with a three-inch cannon, the sub surrendered. Coast Guard cutters also captured German U-boats during the war.[10] U-boats, or submarines, got their name from the German *unter wasser*, meaning *under water*.

In 1943 and 1944, the Coast Guard made history by using helicopters to rescue people at sea for the very first time. As mentioned earlier, Coast Guardsmen served as crews on more than 1,400 ships during the war, including 351 navy vessels and 288 army vessels. All together, 966 Coast Guard enlisted men and 72 Coast Guard officers were killed during the war.

Signalman First Class Douglas Munro

Born in Vancouver, British Columbia, Signalman Douglas Munro joined the Coast Guard during World War II. On September 27, 1942, he won the Congressional Medal of Honor for his actions as the commander of twenty-four boats evacuating five hundred wounded marines from the beaches of Guadalcanal, still under the control of the Japanese. Munro commanded the landing craft as they came under fire and used his own boat as a shield from Japanese machine-gun fire so that the other boats to could land and board the marines. He was killed, but the rest of the boat crew, many of them wounded, carried on to complete the evacuation and save the lives of hundreds.

After World War II

Soon after World War II, a Coast Guard advisory group went to Korea to help in the creation of the Korean Coast Guard, which later evolved into the Navy of the Republic of Korea. When war broke out between communist North Korea and democratic South Korea, the United States joined the war on the side of South Korea.

There were 22 Coast Guard cutters in operations in the territorial waters of Korea during the Korean War from 1950 to 1953. Cutters assigned to ocean weather stations provided the United Nations forces with information needed in battle. Cutters also served a communication function and guarded planes, coming to the assistance of crews who needed to be rescued from the sea.

With the buildings of Seoul in the background, crew members of the Coast Guard cutter *Midgett* line the bow during a pass in review in honor of the Republic of Korea. Advisors from the U.S. Coast Guard helped create the Korean Coast Guard, which later became the Korean Navy.

In January 1953, a navy reconnaissance airplane was shot down over the China Sea, and it was a Coast Guard seaplane that rescued survivors, despite having to land in 12-foot seas. On take-off, one of the seaplane's engines failed, and the plane crashed. Though he was injured, the pilot, Coast Guard Lieutenant John Vukic, helped most of the survivors out of the plane and onto life rafts. A surface vessel picked up the survivors the following day. Five Coast Guardsmen lost their lives during the rescue. Coast Guard personnel also manned Long Range Aids to Navigation stations (LORAN) throughout the Pacific.

Once the situation in Korea was resolved by a peace treaty, the Coast Guard resumed its peacetime role, being responsible mainly for vessels' safe operation on American waters. During the 1960s and 1970s, Coast Guard crews were assigned to navy ships.

The U.S. Coast Guard must protect the nation's water from pollution. Checking the coastline for contamination helps protect both people and animals from hazardous waste products.

Coast Guard vessels patrolled the territorial waters of North and South Vietnam during the Vietnam War.

In 1967, Congress passed legislation stating that in time of peace the Coast Guard cutter service would no longer form part of the Treasury Department but fall under the auspices of the new Department of Transportation. Since then the peacetime Coast Guard has experienced dramatic changes in its duties of law enforcement related to illegal drugs, pollution of the environment, and illegal immigration.

Coast Guard ships have the double duty of stopping and saving many would-be immigrants who try to enter the United States illegally each year. The Coast Guard frequently rescues these people as their unseaworthy and often overcrowded rafts sink beneath them as they make their way to the United States. At the same time that the Coast Guard is performing this lifesaving mission, it is also charged with guarding these illegal immigrants and turning them over to the Immigration and Naturalization Service in order to return them to their country of origin.[11]

Today the Coast Guard has more than 80,000 personnel, including 38,000 on active duty, 8,000 Reservists, and 35,000 members of Coast Guard Auxiliaries as well as civilian employees. Coast Guardsmen patrol the nation's shores and waterways, increasing marine safety and protecting the environment. At the same time, the Coast Guard works hand in hand with the United States Navy in joint operations around the world.

People of the Coast Guard

Today about eighty thousand men and women serve in the U.S. Coast Guard. All volunteer to serve; none are drafted. They work both on shore and at sea in many different kinds of Coast Guard stations, including lighthouses, rescue aircraft fields, and deep-diving retrieval ships. Coast Guard personnel are posted all over the United States. Some also go overseas. Enlisted personnel work in offices as well as on the decks of seagoing ships, while others man harbor stations and tugboats closer to home.

Not everybody who works for the Coast Guard serves in uniform every day. The Coast Guard depends on the eight thousand members of its standby force, the Coast Guard Reserve, who are trained and paid to

One of the Coast Guard's duties is to patrol United States waters. Coast Guardsmen must always watch for any problems such as stranded boats, injured people, or illegal activities.

step in and perform many duties at a moment's notice. Almost all of the members of the Coast Guard Reserve work at regular civilian jobs and live with their families during most of the year. Reservists train one weekend a month and several weeks each year. Besides the paid members of the Coast Guard, there are thousands of Coast Guard Auxiliaries, both men and women, who live throughout the country and volunteer their time to perform needed Coast Guard–related tasks. The Coast Guard also employs some civilians—individuals and companies—to perform maintenance and repairs at bases and harbors around the country.

Life in the Coast Guard differs in many ways from regular civilian life. Even though their agency falls under the direction of the United States Department of Transportation, Coast Guard personnel have a military lifestyle similar in many respects to that of the United States Navy. Military life is highly ordered. Most things are done in a certain way and at a certain time. When they are on active duty, members of the Coast Guard dress in uniforms. Their haircuts and personal accessories, such as jewelry, have to conform to regulations. In terms of behavior, they are expected to maintain discipline and obey orders. Members of the Coast Guard are always ready to work overtime for long periods, especially when emergencies arise, such as rescues. Often Coast Guard personnel work under dangerous conditions in their efforts to protect or save the lives and property of others.

Despite the regimentation and the risks they must take, Coast Guardsmen generally love their lifestyle and the work they do. Their jobs require special skills and are often challenging and exciting. The Coast Guard is an especially good career choice for people who love boats and who enjoy spending time on and around the water. Advantages of joining the Coast Guard include good pay, benefits, and job security. The Coast

Many small and large ships get caught in severe storms while at sea. The Coast Guard must be prepared to respond to any call for help, no matter how rough and dangerous the water is.

Guard offers its personnel additional educational opportunities and training. Although most people choose to leave the Coast Guard once their enlistment contract expires, many stay for more than twenty years of service—the required number of years to qualify for retirement benefits.[1]

Recruitment

Coast Guard recruiting offices exist all over the nation. Two Coast Guard recruiters and a civilian assistant staff a typical recruiting office. They readily answer the questions of anyone who comes to the office, and the recruiters regularly visit local high schools to give informational presentations about Coast Guard life and to talk to interested high school students. Coast Guard recruiters also attend local area job fairs and compete for the

Being in the Coast Guard means working with state-of-the-art equipment, such as these helicopters: the HH-3F "Pelican" (below) and the HH-65A "Dolphin" (right).

best and the brightest young high school graduates who do not plan to attend a college immediately. The Coast Guard is also interested in individuals who are already attending college; recruiters regularly give presentations to them about the benefits of a career as an officer in the Coast Guard.

Eligibility

The Coast Guard will accept an application from any American citizen or legal immigrant with permanent resident status who is at least seventeen years old but has not yet reached his or her twenty-eighth birthday.[2] The Coast Guard prefers applicants who have graduated from high school or who have obtained a high school equivalency degree, or GED. Recruits have to meet minimum physical requirements that include height, weight, and vision standards. The Coast Guard offers enlistment contracts to applicants who:

- Meet the academic and physical requirements stated above

- Possess a high moral character

- Receive at least the minimum required score on the Armed Services Vocational Aptitude Battery.

This series, or battery, of tests measures the applicants' skills in mathematics and language. In addition, the battery contains aptitude tests that are designed to reveal applicants' natural interests and abilities. The results of this battery of tests are used to help place recruits in a particular training program and a type of work that each recruit is suited for and that each recruit would enjoy.

Commander Melville B. Guttormsen

Commander Melville B. Guttormsen had more than forty-five years of service in the Coast Guard as of June 30, 1999, when he retired. Guttormsen joined the Coast Guard as an enlisted man in October, 1954. He became an officer in 1973. From 1990 until his retirement, Commander Guttormsen had the honor of being the Coast Guard's Gold Ancient Mariner, the person with the most active duty time in service. During his career at sea, Guttormsen served aboard eight different cutters. In 1991, he was the executive officer, second in command, of the cutter *Tamaroa*, which conducted rescue operations during one of the worst winter storms of the decade.

Contracts

Once eligibility has been established, recruiters offer applicants a contract. Enlistment contracts specify the length of time a recruit will serve on active duty. In addition, Coast Guard contracts usually state that personnel are required to serve in the Reserves for a year or two after completing their active duty enlistment. In an individual's contract, the Coast Guard commits to the recruit's job, rating and pay, the benefits he or she will receive, and the occupational training and continuing education opportunities he or she is guaranteed. In addition to their pay, members of the military receive free room and board or a housing and subsistence allowance, medical and dental care, and a military clothing allowance. All members of the Coast Guard accumulate thirty days of vacation, or leave, each year.[3]

Boot Camp

After enlisting, new recruits are sent for at least eight weeks of boot camp. Boot camp takes place at the Coast Guard Training Facility in Cape May, New Jersey. Some training takes place in classrooms, where recruits get instruction in subjects like first aid, fire fighting, weapons handling, and seamanship. Every day recruits also undergo tough physical fitness training. At the swimming pool they learn water survival and rescue techniques. Aboard ship, recruits learn the rules of how to get around as well as the names for the many strange new tools and machines

The Coast Guard calls all boats over 65 feet "cutters." There are three types of cutters: the 378-foot "Hamilton" class, the 270-foot "Reliance" class, and the 210-foot "Reliance" class. Cutters transport crews all over the U.S. waterways and to other countries.

that exist aboard a ship. They also learn what to do if there is an emergency aboard ship and how to survive in the event the ship sinks. If, at the end of boot camp, recruits fail the Coast Guard's physical fitness test, the swimming test, or a written academic exam, they spend more time in boot camp. Individuals who prove to be discipline problems during boot camp are usually discharged.

Additional Training

At the end of boot camp, some enlisted personnel are immediately assigned to a duty station ashore or on a ship. In an apprentice-type system, new Guardsmen learn their jobs by following the directions of more experienced seamen. In this way, they learn the job by doing it. Soon, however, the apprentice becomes the master of the job and is assigned to teach others. The Coast Guard warns recruits early on that anyone who gets assigned to a unit with a galley right out of boot camp starts out as a mess cook for a month or so. During this period of additional training, however, Coast Guardsmen also learn about the ship they are assigned to. Those who are assigned to a shore station learn about the boats they will use for their work at the station. Soon they may get assigned to help with rescue missions, assist with law enforcement, or work on aids to navigation systems, depending on the primary mission their unit fulfills.

Recruits who have been selected at enlistment to fill highly technical jobs do not go directly to duty stations when they graduate from boot camp. After a short leave, they are assigned to one of the many technical schools that the Coast Guard and other military services maintain around the country. The Coast Guard calls these schools "A-schools." Students are instructed in the basic knowledge and the technical skills required in such fields as electronics, navigation, sonar, and even record keeping. The Coast Guard has devoted much time to make its schools the best—using the best possible ways to teach the highly complex skills that are needed to run its modern ships and

The first responsibility of the United States Coast Guard is to keep people safe on the nation's waters. Here the crew of a Coast Guard helicopter transfers an injured man to a waiting ambulance.

aircraft. A-schools are highly respected in the civilian world. A person who has graduated from one usually has little trouble getting a highly paid civilian job after completing his or her enlistment. Once seamen graduate from an A-school, they are usually given a promotion and assigned to a duty station ashore or aboard ship. The new graduates continue to learn through the apprentice system, where their new "book knowledge" is put to work in everyday situations.

Promotions and Ranks

Enlisted Coast Guard personnel get promoted for length of service, good performance, and completion of certain levels of training. Promotions include increases in pay. The table on the following page lists the various titles and ranks of enlisted Coast Guard personnel along with the specific requirements, or qualifications, for each. Comments provide additional information.

Officer Candidate School

Regular enlisted Coast Guard personnel who have earned a college degree and desire to become commissioned officers can apply for admission to the Coast Guard Officer Candidate School in New London, Connecticut. Competition for admission is very tough. Applicants must meet age and medical requirements. Candidates who are accepted attend the school for seventeen weeks of training. They take courses in

Enlisted Coast Guard Ranks			
Title	**Rank**	**Qualification**	**Comment**
Seaman Recruit	E-1	At enlistment.	
Seaman Apprentice	E-2	End of boot camp.	
Seaman	E-3	After several months of regular duty.	
Third Class Petty Officer	E-4	Recommendation of a superior officer or graduation from some A-schools.	Seaman must have gained knowledge and experience valuable to the Coast Guard.
Second Class Petty Officer	E-5	Service-wide examinations and the requirements of the specific duty stations.	Each step beyond third class petty officer requires more time in service, passing an exam, and a higher standard of character and competency.
First Class Petty Officer	E-6		
Chief Petty Officer	E-7		*Note: A master chief petty officer is indeed a master of his or her skills, with probably more than 15 years of service.*
Senior Petty Officer	E-8		
Master Chief Petty Officer	E-9		

leadership, nautical science, law enforcement, and seamanship. Candidates also spend about two weeks under way aboard one of the Coast Guard cutters for first-hand experience. Those who complete the course of study successfully and graduate receive commissions as ensigns in the Coast Guard. The new officers initially sign a contract for three years of active duty. When their contracts are completed, some officers are given the opportunity to continue their careers as regular commissioned officers in the Coast Guard.

In addition to the regular Officer Candidate School (OCS) course, the Coast Guard conducts an

All Coast Guard servicemen and servicewomen need to know where they are while at sea. Learning to chart a course may save their lives one day. At one of the many technical schools maintained by the Coast Guard, students learn such skills as navigation.

Officer Indoctrination School (OIS). The OIS is open to all Coast Guard warrant officers and junior officers from other foreign and civilian maritime services. OIS and OCS students attend all classes together. Upon graduation, Coast Guard warrant officers with over two years' commissioned service receive commissions

Highly trained Coast Guard personnel support combat troops in other branches of the U.S. armed forces. These radiomen 2nd class are working in an explosives ordnance center during Operation Desert Shield in the Middle East.

as lieutenants (junior grade). Warrant officers with less than two years' commissioned service are commissioned as ensigns.[4] The table on the following page shows the order of ranks for warrant officers and commissioned officers.

The Coast Guard Academy

The Coast Guard Academy was founded in 1876 with a class of nine students on board the Revenue cutter *Dobbin*. In 1932, a permanent Academy was built on land along the Thames River donated by the New London, Connecticut, community. Unlike the other service academies, the Coast Guard does not require a

Officer-Level Coast Guard Ranks
Warrant Officers
Chief Warrant Officer 2
Chief Warrant Officer 3
Chief Warrant Officer 4
Commissioned Officers
Ensign
Lieutenant, junior grade
Lieutenant
Lieutenant Commander
Commander
Captain
Rear Admiral (lower half)
Rear Admiral (upper half)
Vice Admiral
Admiral (Commandant)

congressional appointment to enter the Academy. All applicants who are accepted receive full scholarships. Admission to the Academy is based on nationwide competition. Each year approximately 5,500 candidates apply for 225 seats in each class. Applicants must be United States citizens, either born or naturalized. They must be unmarried and have no dependents, and they must be between seventeen and twenty-two years old. Candidates must also pass a medical exam. In addition, they must be high school graduates who have completed either the SAT I (Scholastic

Second-class cadets aboard the Coast Guard cutter *Eagle* learn navigation along with other skills.

Assessment Test) or the ACT (American College Test). All students attending the Academy are required to live in Academy living quarters. Cadets complete a regular college education to earn a Bachelor of Science (BS) degree, and they are commissioned as ensigns in the Coast Guard at graduation. Each graduate is required to serve a period of five years of active duty.

Coast Guard Academy resources include the library, which houses 150,000 volumes, 600 periodicals, and an Online Public Access Catalog. Laboratories are maintained for

The U.S. Coast Guard cutter *Eagle* may look old-fashioned, but it is actually a Coast Guard training vessel. Cadets use the ship in training missions all over the world.

Cadets from the U.S. Coast Guard Academy present a sharp appearance in their dress uniforms, known as "salt and peppers."

physics, chemistry, computers, oceanography, electronics, navigation, and engineering experimentation and analysis. The Academy also has a Bridge/Combat Information Center simulator, a radar trainer, 65-foot training vessels, and the 295-foot sailing ship *Eagle*.

The Coast Guard Academy is the smallest of all the nation's military academies. In 1999, with a total of only 850 cadets, the Academy made military history when the cadet regimental staff (student officers) became 60 percent female, including six women and four men. One of the women, Cadet First Class Peggy M. Gross, was regimental commander. That year, one-third of the entire student body was female. This represented a big increase since 1992, when women made up less than 25 percent of the school.[5]

In addition to having a very demanding academic schedule, cadets receive training each summer. Freshman year at the Academy begins in July,

Each summer, cadets receive training on different types of boats in preparation for shipboard life after they graduate.

seven weeks prior to the academic school year. The first seven weeks, known as "Swab Summer," are an invigorating period of physical, military, and leadership training. The last week is spent sailing aboard the Coast Guard sailing ship *Eagle*. Cadets spend five weeks of their sophomore summer sailing on board the *Eagle*, three weeks at a Coast Guard unit, and two weeks sailing small boats. Junior summer includes training in leadership, shipboard routines, rifle and pistol, and aviation. In preparation for shipboard life after graduation, seniors spend ten weeks aboard a Coast Guard cutter learning the roles they will be responsible for as junior officers.[6]

Officers' Benefits

Career Coast Guard officers enjoy most of the same benefits as their counterparts in the other military services. Exciting work, regular advances in salary and responsibility, a chance to see the world, equal treatment regardless of race or gender, and thirty days of paid vacation each year are attractive benefits for any career. In addition to benefits just mentioned, Coast Guard officers have access to recreational facilities, officer's clubs, and the Postgraduate Educational Program, through which they can earn postgraduate degrees.

The Coast Guard Reserve

Like other branches of the military, the Coast Guard backs up its active duty force with a reserve force of well-trained personnel. Members of the Coast Guard Reserve live most of the year as civilians. Reservists work one weekend every month and two weeks during the year in the active branch of the Coast Guard so that they can maintain and update their skills and knowledge. When on active duty, 85 percent of reservists work alongside active duty Coast Guard personnel, and 80 percent of their time is spent on the job. In this way they contribute more than 300,000 days of work each year. The Coast Guard recognizes the importance of a strong Reserve, so in 1999 it increased its advertising budget from $35,000 to $2 million in order to attract more and better applicants.

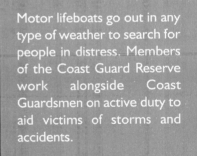

Motor lifeboats go out in any type of weather to search for people in distress. Members of the Coast Guard Reserve work alongside Coast Guardsmen on active duty to aid victims of storms and accidents.

The Coast Guard Auxiliary

The Coast Guard Auxiliary is composed of over thirty thousand men and women who have an interest in boating safety. These men and women donate their time to help the Coast Guard perform all of its duties related to safe boating. Members of the Auxiliary give boating safety courses at local schools and marinas. They conduct examinations for boating safety equipment such as life preservers and fire extinguishers on the country's rivers and lakes. Their instruction of and work with boaters is extremely important. In 1998 alone, the Coast Guard Auxiliary saved 445 lives. Today, members of the Auxiliary also serve the Coast Guard as interpreters at foreign conferences and meetings.[7]

Structure of the Coast Guard

Coast Guard History

As the first chart on the following pages shows, the evolution of the United States Coast Guard followed the development of five separate services. At the initiation of each service, the individual service was responsible for certain duties. However, as the years passed, the functions, or duties, of the various services expanded and often overlapped.

On January 28, 1915, the Revenue Cutter Service and the Life-Saving Service were joined to form the United States Coast Guard. Then, in 1939, the existing Lighthouse Service was made part of the Coast Guard Service. Finally, on February 28, 1942, the Bureau of Navigation and Steamboat Inspection, which had functioned as two separate services—the

Steamboat Inspection Service and the Bureau of Navigation—was also made part of the U.S. Coast Guard.

Coast Guard Organization

The second chart shows how the Coast Guard is organized. The chain of command goes from the president of the United States, who is the commander in chief (not shown), to the Commandant and Vice Commandant of the Coast Guard. They are in charge of the five districts in the Atlantic area and the four districts in the Pacific area as well as the Chief of Staff. In turn, the Chief of Staff oversees several groups, or directorates, as shown.

Coast Guard Budget

The third chart shows how the Coast Guard budget for 2001 is broken down between expenditures for the Coast Guard's different responsibilities. Amounts shown are in millions of dollars.

Coast Guard History[1]

The Lighthouse Service—1789
Recognizing the importance of safe waterways to the commerce of a growing nation, Congress created the Lighthouse Service to ensure a coordinated system of aids to navigation.

The Revenue Cutter Service—1790
Secretary of the Treasury Alexander Hamilton asked Congress for 10 ships to enforce the tariffs necessary to repay the young country's massive debts from the Revolutionary War.

Steamboat Inspection Service—1838
Congress created the service to answer growing public concern over boiler explosions on the unregulated steamboat fleet. The service inspected hulls and machinery and licensed engineers.

U.S. Life-Saving Service—1848
After a number of tragic shipwrecks, Congress created a series of stations along America's waterways with crews ready to respond to any mariner in distress.

Bureau of Navigation—1884
The bureau was created to administer the nation's navigation laws, which were increasing during this time in response to growing merchant traffic and international efforts to standardize safety at sea.

The U.S. Coast Guard—1915
In an effort to reduce government bureaucracy, the earlier services were combined into a single military organization—the Coast Guard. The Coast Guard has continued all of the missions for which its predecessor agencies were created and has acquired many new missions in this century.

Organization of the Coast Guard[2]

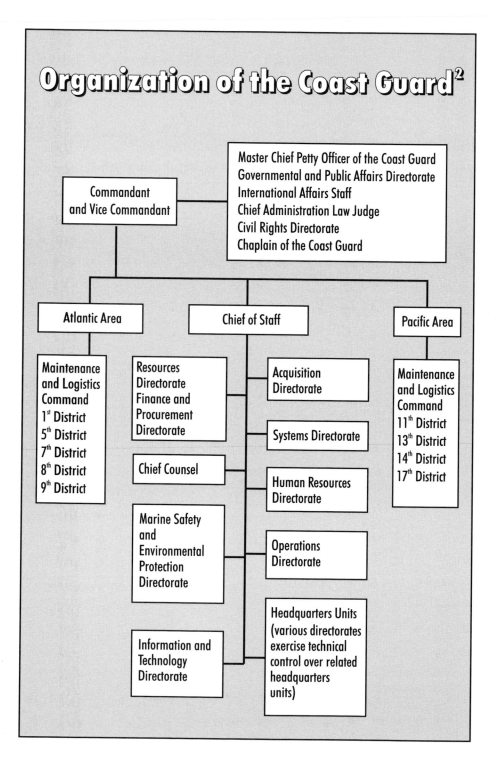

Commandant and Vice Commandant

- Master Chief Petty Officer of the Coast Guard
- Governmental and Public Affairs Directorate
- International Affairs Staff
- Chief Administration Law Judge
- Civil Rights Directorate
- Chaplain of the Coast Guard

Atlantic Area

Maintenance and Logistics Command
1st District
5th District
7th District
8th District
9th District

Chief of Staff

Resources Directorate Finance and Procurement Directorate

Chief Counsel

Marine Safety and Environmental Protection Directorate

Information and Technology Directorate

Acquisition Directorate

Systems Directorate

Human Resources Directorate

Operations Directorate

Headquarters Units (various directorates exercise technical control over related headquarters units)

Pacific Area

Maintenance and Logistics Command
11th District
13th District
14th District
17th District

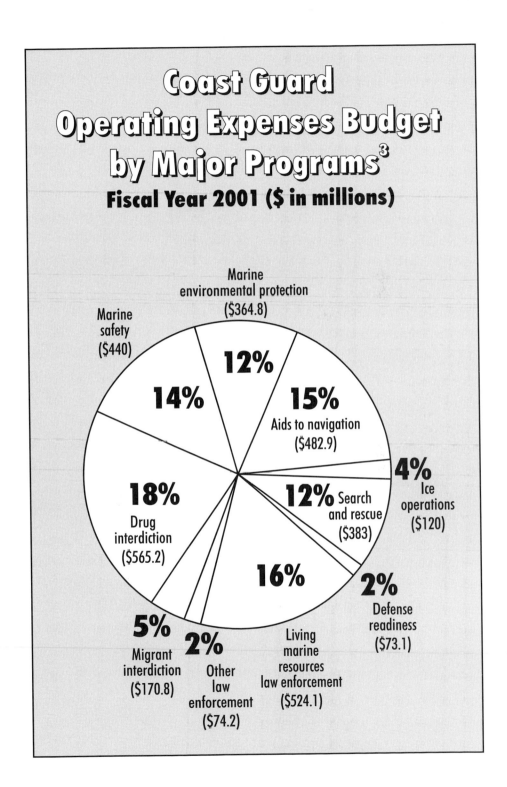

Coast Guard Operating Expenses Budget by Major Programs[3]
Fiscal Year 2001 ($ in millions)

Marine environmental protection ($364.8) — 12%

Marine safety ($440) — 14%

Aids to navigation ($482.9) — 15%

Ice operations ($120) — 4%

Search and rescue ($383) — 12%

Defense readiness ($73.1) — 2%

Drug interdiction ($565.2) — 18%

Living marine resources law enforcement ($524.1) — 16%

Migrant interdiction ($170.8) — 5%

Other law enforcement ($74.2) — 2%

Duties of the Coast Guard

The Coast Guard has the duty to protect American lives and property at sea, to defend the nation's coastlines, and to enforce navigation, immigration, and customs laws. In performing these duties, the Coast Guard operates many different kinds of ships, called cutters, and also many different small boats, from harbor tugs to river patrol boats equipped with outboard motors. Each of these missions, or duties, requires many different skills, ranging from sheer physical strength and courage to the knowledge of and ability to use sophisticated computer programs, and a little of everything in between. Although the Coast Guard has many duties, its primary mission is to rescue people in need. A Coast Guard officer serving as a harbor administrator may not seem obvious, but most people would recognize a Coast Guard rescue helicopter when it is filmed hovering over a disabled ship and shown on the TV evening news.

Search and Rescue

In a typical year during the 1990s, the Coast Guard received more than sixty thousand calls for assistance and made about six thousand rescues.[1] One kind of distress call that the Coast Guard answers comes from commercial ships and fishing boats many miles out to sea. Offshore fishing can be very dangerous. In just the month of May 1999, there were ten commercial fishing boats sunk and eleven people either missing or known dead. That month may have been especially costly, but every month there are always wrecks, collisions, and missing people.[2]

Quickly locating a vessel that requires assistance is an important part of any successful rescue operation.

The National Distress System is a Coast Guard–operated system of radio networks that cover the entire U.S. coastline and the waters 20 miles off its shore. The Coast Guard is currently updating this coverage to make use of

Helicopters are important in Coast Guard search and rescue efforts. Helicopters can lower crew members to a ship in a bucket. When all the stranded people have been rescued, they are flown to safety.

Sometimes the Coast Guard's search and rescue missions are a bit unusual. Here a helicopter swoops down to rescue three balloonists who crashed into the Pacific Ocean during an unsuccessful attempt to circle the globe.

the latest satellite, radar, and radio technology to be able to pinpoint the scene of a disaster as soon as possible after any contact is made. In 1999, the Maritime Differential Global Positioning System went into operation. This system can accurately locate a vessel in distress within a range of five meters anywhere on the world's oceans.

In such an emergency, distressed vessels must be able to notify possible rescuers that help is needed, and they must be able to guide the rescuers to their distressed vessel. Voice radio is the "notifier" of choice. It can also help locate a vessel if two radio direction finders monitor the signal.[3] Under Coast Guard regulations, all commercial vessels have to carry a "smart" Emergency Position Indicating Radio

Beacon. This is a self-contained, floating radio transmitter that will transmit details about a particular boat and its location. Also, the Coast Guard has approved a distress flag. It shows a black square and a black ball set side by side in the center of an orange background. Finally, the Coast Guard certifies life rafts, which need to be inspected periodically at a Coast Guard–approved inspection station.[4]

Enforcing Regulations

Lifesaving and icebreaking may be considered glamorous parts of the Coast Guard's mission to protect American ships and property. A number of other Coast Guard functions may not seem quite so glamorous, but they play an important part in preventing accidents at sea and in the ports and harbors along the coasts and the inland waterways of the United States.

The Coast Guard is responsible for enforcing the rules and regulations of the United States government for its harbors and territorial waters. The Coast Guard makes the rules that govern how ships must operate in the territorial waters of the United States. Some of these rules are designed to ensure the safety of the people who crew the ships. For example, there are rules that state how many people may work on board vessels of given sizes. They also spell out what safety equipment vessels must carry. Some regulations are designed to protect the environment, such as a prohibition against pumping out sewage and water collected in the bilge (the lowest part of the ship's hull) within harbors and inland waterways.

Environment

The Coast Guard takes a more direct hand in protecting the environment when it responds to crises like oil spills. A massive oil spill near Valdez, Alaska, on March 24, 1989, caused the pollution of miles of Alaskan coastline and the death of thousands of seabirds and mammals. A painful lesson was learned from that disaster and the long, hard cleanup that followed. The destructive force of petroleum products on the environment can be enormous, and it can take years to repair such damage.

Today, the Coast Guard stands ready to combat such environmental disasters around the globe. On February 4, 1999, the 639-foot merchant vessel *New Caris*, registered in Panama, went aground off the coast of Coos Bay, Oregon, carrying nearly 400,000 gallons of fuel oil. Winds greater than 60 miles per hour along with 35-foot waves battered the hull of the *New Caris* against the rocks. The Coast Guard quickly began efforts to salvage the ship and recover the spilled oil. At the same time, the Coast Guard organized other agencies to begin a beach cleanup and a wildlife-rescue operation.

Afraid that the *New Caris* would completely break apart, the Coast Guard set most of the hull and its oil spill on fire. Coast Guard cutters towed the 420-foot bow section with 140,000 gallons of oil still aboard

Pollution destroys the habitat of marine animals and the beautiful beaches that people enjoy. It can take years to repair the damage caused by some types of pollution. The Coast Guard plays an important role in combating environmental disasters.

over 240 miles to a deep-sea grave location. The bow section was then torpedoed, and it sank, carrying its cargo of oil to an 11,000-foot grave. There the water temperature hovered near freezing and kept the oil inert and trapped within the wrecked hull. Recently the Coast Guard has equipped oceangoing buoy tenders with pollution response capability that will quickly alert monitors ashore when excessive pollution appears in the water.

Recreational Boating

The Coast Guard oversees recreational boating-safety regulations. Many Americans love boats, and as a result, one-quarter of the country's population spends some of its free time boating. In the United States, there are 16 million boats! Boaters face all kinds of emergencies. For example, a boat engine may catch fire, or a vessel might capsize. Careless or reckless boaters often speed dangerously and endanger nearby swimmers as well as other boaters. Passengers without life jackets fall overboard and drown.

More people die every year in boating accidents than in airplane crashes. Also, approximately five thousand people are seriously injured every year in boating accidents. To help prepare boaters for emergencies, the Coast Guard offers boating-safety classes, and the Coast Guard Auxiliary administers Courtesy Marine Examinations. The Coast Guard has also developed basic standards for safe boating. It has issued regulations concerning safe-boat designs and the safety equipment that should be installed or carried on board every vessel, including fire extinguishers, life jackets, signaling devices, radios, and running lights.

Federal regulations state that boats measuring less than 20 feet long must have enough flotation to support a swamped hull, all installed machinery and fuel, and as many passengers as the boat has capacity for. There are formulas for calculating this,

Not all Coast Guard craft are large and powerful. Since personal watercraft are small, fast, and easy to maneuver, they are an efficient way for Coast Guardsmen to watch the harbor's pleasure and commercial boats and come to their aid if necessary.

and all boats in production today are sold with a capacity plate, stating the boat's capacity according to U.S. Coast Guard safety standards. A boat's speed rates are posted near the operator's position. These rates, based on testing, indicate the speed at which maneuverability will become difficult and therefore unsafe. Just as for the large oceangoing vessels, there are requirements regarding the discharge of waste material from small boats' toilets and bilges.

As a preventive measure, the Coast Guard maintains a list of problems that might be experienced with various boat models. One public service offered

Motor lifeboats are the most common type of rescue boat. Here the crews of a motor lifeboat and a motor surfboat train off the coast of Cape Disappointment, Washington.

by both the Coast Guard and its Auxiliary is free safety inspection of boats. Potential boat buyers can ask the Coast Guard to do a safety inspection of a boat they wish to buy (permission from the present owner is required). In addition, boat owners can have their boats periodically inspected, just for safety's sake.

The Coast Guard has the right to stop and board any boat at any time. They can charge an owner with hazardous operations like speeding. On board, the Coast Guard can search for contraband, check for safety violations, and inspect documents and papers. Coast Guard inspectors stop about eighty-five

One of the Coast Guard's missions is to protect all people on the water. Over ninety Coast Guard Auxiliary boats were on patrol during the OpSail 2000 parade of tall ships in New York harbor.

thousand vessels each year. In half of these situations, they find some violations of boating regulations. In extreme cases, boats are ordered to return to port or they are seized.

In terms of boater education, the Coast Guard faces a particularly difficult challenge. For example, an individual who operates a motor vehicle or flies an airplane is required to receive some training and to be licensed. There are no standards to determine who can operate a boat. The Coast Guard Auxiliary tries to educate boaters to operate their boats safely. The Auxiliary offers courses on boating skills, seamanship, and coastal navigation. Every month it publishes the *Boating Safety Circular*.[5]

Immigration

Another of the Coast Guard's responsibilities is illegal immigration. The Coast Guard continually patrols coastal waters looking for boats carrying people who are attempting to enter the country illegally. Cubans, Dominicans, and Haitians come to the United States in the largest numbers in this way. In 1997, the Coast Guard intercepted a Haitian freighter that had almost completed the 600-mile journey from Haiti to Miami Beach, Florida. The Coast Guard cutter on patrol dispatched four boarding parties in small boats to inspect the ship. The freighter quickly sped away to try to escape the small boats. When a larger Coast Guard cutter overtook the Haitian freighter, it surrendered immediately. It was a harrowing experience. All of the immigrants were safely taken back to Haiti, except for one woman who was hospitalized for dehydration.[6]

For years, illegal immigration to the United States from Cuba has been a major concern of the Coast Guard. Until 1994, almost any Cuban who made it to the shores of Florida was accepted as a legal immigrant. Since then, the United States has followed several policies regarding Cuban refugees. On August 22, 1994, the Coast Guard picked up twenty-five hundred Cubans at sea. Some were returned to Cuba, and some were allowed to stay in the United States.

It is not up to the Coast Guard to determine what is done with illegal immigrants who are stopped from entering the United States. Regardless of the outcome,

the Coast Guard is directed to stop illegal immigrants and keep them alive and healthy until other branches of the United States government determine their fate.

In August of 1998, a Coast Guard C-130 aircraft on patrol sighted a suspicious 180-foot Chinese fishing vessel 150 miles southwest of Baja California. The Coast Guard sent a cutter, the 378-foot long *Munro*, which found 172 illegal Chinese immigrants in the holds of the vessel. The Coast Guard shipped more than 40,000 pounds of supplies to these needy immigrants before their vessel was towed to San Diego, California. The Coast Guard stopped more than 240 Chinese immigrants from illegally entering the country during 1998. That year the Coast Guard stopped a total of 3,600 illegal immigrants from coming into the United States. The vast majority of these immigrants were from the islands of the

Above: Every year many people from all over the world try to enter the United States. Some cross the treacherous ocean in makeshift rafts. The Coast Guard is always watching for these illegal aliens. When they are found, the Coast Guard must often rescue them.

Left: Haitians who tried to enter the United States illegally wait aboard a Coast Guard boat before being returned to Port-au-Prince, Haiti. The largest numbers of illegal aliens picked up by the Coast Guard come from Haiti, Cuba, and the Dominican Republic.

Caribbean, and they were trying to enter the country through the state of Florida.

Customs

Coast Guard vessels and airplanes work hard to stop drug traffic on the seas. The Coast Guard regularly patrols for drug runners throughout the Caribbean, the eastern Pacific Ocean, and the Gulf of Mexico. Closer to home, patrols are made along the nation's coasts and up and down the nation's inland water-ways.[7] Coast Guard personnel have the authority to seize vessels on which they find any illegal drugs. Drug smugglers often try to outrun the Coast Guard patrols.

A 40-foot boat, powered by two 250-horsepower engines and manned by two or three men, can travel more than 50 miles per hour, carrying more than a ton of cocaine. With the aid of night-vision goggles, satellite phones, and digital precision location equipment, smugglers run past even the fastest Coast Guard boats. In recent years, smugglers along the coasts of Mexico and other Caribbean locales would simply ignore Coast Guard patrol aircraft flying overhead

Left: Besides looking for boats in trouble, the Coast Guard looks for boats causing trouble. Many people try to bring contraband (illegal items) into the United States by boat. The Coast Guard searches suspicious boats and seizes illegal goods.

Below: The Coast Guard uses patrol craft in its efforts to stem the flow of illegal drugs into the United States. These boats are equipped with advanced electronics and communications equipment as well as satellite navigation equipment.

because they could easily finish their business and get away long before any Coast Guard boats could arrive. Recently the Coast Guard has authorized the use of MH-90 Enforcer armed helicopters capable of using nonlethal force, warning shots, and, if necessary, disabling fire to combat even the fastest drug boats. These attack helicopters are based on nearby helicopter carrier ships and can overtake any boat at speeds of more than 120 miles per hour. Coast Guard efforts around the island of Puerto Rico in 1997–1998 showed remarkable results. More than 40 ships and

In wartime, the Coast Guard becomes part of the armed forces. This boatswain's mate 3rd class took her post aboard a port security boat as part of Operation Desert Shield, which preceded the Gulf War against Iraq in 1990.

nearly 117,000 pounds of cocaine were seized. Regular crimes as well as drug busts were reduced throughout the island as a result of what experts estimated to be the seizure of one half of the island's regular drug supply.[8]

Military Operations

The Coast Guard is part of the Department of Transportation during peacetime and has its own national security missions, which include national defense maritime safety, maritime law enforcement, and marine environmental protection. When the United States goes to war, the Coast Guard becomes a part of the armed forces, and its operations are directed by the Department of Defense. In the late 1990s, the Coast Guard supported and sometimes led in enforcing United Nations sanctions and international embargoes at sea. In the North Arabian Sea, Coast Guard vessels enforced United Nations sanctions against Iraq. Other Coast Guard personnel operated aboard navy vessels. The Coast Guard cooperated with the navy to defend and operate shipping in foreign harbors in order to ensure that military equipment arrived safely in those strategic ports.[9]

Women and Minorities in the Coast Guard

Women

Although women did not formally enter the Coast Guard until World War I, there are examples of their involvement with the Coast Guard and earlier groups that later became part of the present-day Coast Guard. For example, in 1791 Mary Lee aided the Revenue Service. She had been hired by a shipping company to protect the cannons that had been purchased for the Revenue cutter *Scammel*. Six smugglers tried to steal the guns before they could be loaded onto the ship, but Mary Lee scared them off. The *Scammel* set sail on schedule thanks to her efforts.

Women have helped run lighthouses since colonial times. Some lighthouse keepers owned female slaves who helped keep the signal lights burning. Others were aided by their wives or their daughters. In Scituate, Massachusetts, Rebecca and Abigail Bates helped their father at his lighthouse. In this way they came to play a role in the War of 1812. In 1814, when the Bates girls spied a British warship entering the Scituate harbor, they picked up fife and drum. To make the British think there was an army regiment posted in the town, the girls started to play a military march. The ruse worked, and the ship turned around and headed back out to sea.

By the mid-nineteenth century, a few women had received appointments as lighthouse keepers. Two

Since the early days of this county, women have helped maintain lighthouses along the coasts of the United States and aided in rescue efforts. Women played an important role in the Lighthouse Service and the Revenue Marine Service, organizations that later became part of the Coast Guard.

examples are Ida Lewis and Harriet Colfax. Ida was so famous her face appeared on the cover of *Harper's Weekly* in 1869, and Harriet "manned" the Michigan City Lighthouse from 1861 to 1904.[1] The Service gave its Silver Life Saving Medal to Edith Morgan, whose father was in charge of the U.S. Life-Saving Station, Grand Point au Sable, in Hamlin, Michigan. Twice Edith rescued sailors. Once she stood on the shore for six hours in eighteen inches of snow as she hauled survivors ashore with a life rope. Another time she rowed a surfboat out to pick up survivors.

World War I

When the United States entered World War I in 1917, all branches of the military experienced a great need for more personnel. At that time women were allowed to serve in the Navy Reserve. These women worked in noncombat positions such as typists and bookkeepers, thus allowing men to serve in combat positions where they were needed. Soon the Coast Guard followed the navy's example and allowed women to fill similar positions. Genevieve and Lucille Baker, nineteen-year-old twins from Brooklyn, New York, were the first to enlist in the Naval Coast Defense Reserve. They worked as bookkeepers. Other women worked for the Coast Guard as clerks, translators, and radio operators during World War I. All Yeomanettes, as women in the Coast Guard were called, were released from service as soon as the war ended in November 1918.

World War II and the Formation of the SPARs

When the United States entered World War II, all branches of the United States military again experienced a great need for additional personnel. Once again women filled shore jobs. As the men embarked for the field, the women sat down at the typewriters and the radios the men had just left. Eventually, women also went to sea. Congress authorized the creation of the U.S. Coast Guard Women's Reserve on November 23, 1942. Dorothy Stratton, who later became the first director of the Reserve, had suggested a name for this women's division to the commandant just nine days earlier. In a memo, she wrote, "The motto of the Coast Guard is "Semper Paratus—Always Ready." The initials of this motto are, of course, SPAR. Why not call the members of the Women's Reserve SPARs? . . . As I understand it, a spar is often a supporting beam, and that is what we hope each member of the Women's Reserve will be. . . . I like SPAR because it really has meaning."[2]

Some male Coast Guard members had reservations about letting women into the service. However, most male Coast Guard members welcomed the women. The women freed many men from shore work and allowed them to go to sea. Between 1942 and 1946, more than ten thousand women joined the SPARs. When asked why they wanted to join, many women spoke of their desire to contribute to the war effort.

Some mentioned the fact that by doing so they relieved men for active combat. Still others were attracted by opportunities for self-improvement, adventure, and travel that service in the Coast Guard offered. After October 1944, African-American women were accepted into the SPARs. Four African-American women immediately applied and were accepted. The first was Olivia J. Hooker.

The application process involved filling out forms, being interviewed, having a physical examination, and

Women were officially allowed to serve with the Coast Guard during World War I, when they enlisted in the Naval Coast Defense Reserve. Today, women can fill any and all positions in the Coast Guard.

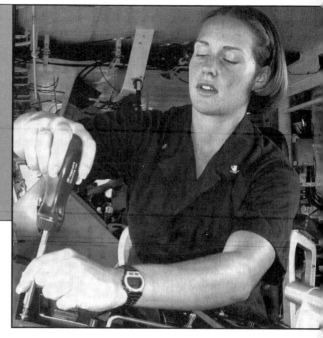

Since being allowed to join the Coast Guard as regular enlistees in 1973, women have made tremendous strides in all branches of the United States armed forces. In the Coast Guard, women continue to give their all to save lives all over the world.

taking a mental apti-
tude test. Most of the
women who applied
already had work
experience as clerks or salespersons. After they were
accepted, recruits were sent to an embarkation point,
and from there they reported to basic training.
The earliest civilian recruits went to a college campus
in Iowa. By the end of the war, all women recruits
underwent basic training at a station in Manhattan
Beach, in New York City, where men also trained. One
special feature of that training station was its dry-land
training ship.

For SPARs, the indoctrination period was a mad
rush of classes, physical education, aptitude tests, physical exams, shots, drill, mess, and watch. Recruits
learned how to stand up straight, how to march in
rank, and how to swab decks in approved seaman fash-
ion. The women were given regulation haircuts and

were issued uniforms. They learned to use nautical terms when talking about everyday activities. For example, all the new SPARs went to "chow," and they referred to 5:30 in the morning, the time they rose, as "0530." After four weeks of intensive training, the recruits took final exams. Those who passed were assigned to units.

The SPARs were demobilized on June 30, 1946. By the end of the war, there were 955 SPAR officers. A few of these women had attended the Coast Guard Academy. Two hundred ninety-nine more had enlisted and then applied for officer training. Most of the other officers had transferred from the U.S. Navy WAVEs. These officers were allowed to keep their commissions when the war ended.

After World War II

The legislation that allowed women into the Coast Guard had provided for their service only through June 30, 1947. A handful of the veteran SPARs were allowed to remain in service after that date, but no new provision was made for women in the service, and those who remained were never promoted. A limited number of SPARs returned to active duty and served during the Korean and Vietnam Wars.[3] In 1973, women were finally allowed to enlist in the U.S. Coast Guard. Soon the Coast Guard Academy became the first service academy to open its doors to women. In 1978, the Coast Guard lifted restrictions dictating which jobs women could fill. In 1985, for the first time, a woman achieved the highest honors among all members of the graduating class at the Coast Guard Academy.[4] Unlike the U.S. Navy, the Coast Guard makes no distinction between men and women in combat. Women can fill any and all positions in the Coast Guard of today.

African Americans

African Americans were among the first people to serve in the Revenue Service when it was founded in 1789. Early in the history of the service, officers sometimes brought their slaves aboard cutters. These slaves served not only as personal servants but also filled the ship's need for stewards, cooks, and ordinary seamen on many Service cutters.

Senegal was a slave who belonged to Hopley

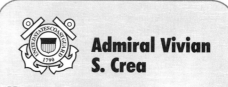

Admiral Vivian S. Crea

Vivian S. Crea, commissioned in 1973, was the first woman aircraft commander in the Coast Guard. She has piloted the C130 Hercules turboprop, the H65 Dolphin helicopter, and the Gulfstream II jet. She was the first female commanding officer of a Coast Guard Air Station when she took command of Air Station Detroit on the Great Lakes. Crea's second command was Air Station Clearwater, the largest air station in the Coast Guard. There she oversaw the 570 personnel who maintain and operate twelve H60 Jayhawk helicopters and seven C130 Hercules aircraft. Today she is Chief of the United States Coast Guard Office of Programs. She is responsible for the Coast Guard's budget development, resource allocation, and program review. Vivian Crea was promoted to admiral in July 1999. She is the first active-duty Coast Guard woman to achieve that rank.

The Coast Guard Academy was the first U.S. military academy to admit women. In addition, the Coast Guard commissions women and men as officers through the College Student Pre-Commissioning Initiative.

Yeaton, the Service's first commissioned officer. Senegal served with distinction on many cruises with Yeaton.

Ironically, a law dated March 22, 1794, prohibited the slave trade between the United States and foreign countries. The Revenue Service was specifically charged with preventing slaves from being imported into the United States. Many of these African-American slaves thus contributed to preventing the importation of any other Africans into the United States from the earliest days of the American antislavery movement. On November 1, 1843, however, a regulation banned slaves from joining the Revenue Service or working on its ships. The measure seems to have been aimed at the actions of the

slave-owning officers in the Revenue Service rather than to have been a comment on the quality of service given by the African Americans.

In 1831, the Treasury Secretary Samuel Ingham authorized the commander of the Revenue cutter *Florida* to take on board his ship a free African-American young man to work as a servant. One month later, another captain was granted permission to employ free African-American men as cooks and stewards. The regular employment of African Americans in all enlisted capacities aboard cutters became normal practice, even after the passage of the regulation prohibiting the service of slaves.[5] It was not until World War II, however, that African Americans were admitted into regular U.S. Coast Guard service.

The Life-Saving Service hired African Americans as U.S. Life-Savers. There were about twenty-five African Americans on the payrolls of Life-Saving Stations in the Fifth and Sixth Coast Guard districts

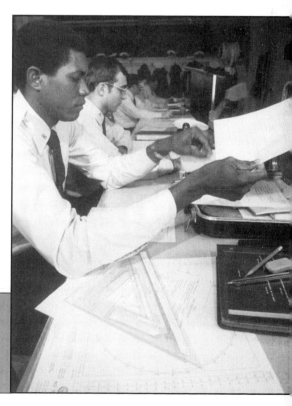

Math class at Officer Candidate School. The Coast Guard of today is committed to racial equality at all levels.

in 1875. In 1878 Richard Etheridge, an African American, became the keeper of the Pea Island, North Carolina, Lifeboat Station. He hired other African Americans as his staff. The staff remained all African-American until 1947, when the station closed.

One of the earliest staff members was Joseph H. Berry, who served for fifteen years. His son, Maxie Berry, Sr., served at the station for twenty-five years. His son, Maxie Berry, Jr., also entered the Coast Guard. He rose to the rank of lieutenant commander.

In 1882 the staff of the Pea Island Station rescued the entire crew of a distressed schooner, the *E. S. Newman*. The schooner had been blown one hundred miles off course in a severe storm and had run aground on a beach two miles south of Etheridge's station. The waters were so rough that the rescue crew could not row out to the ship in their surfboats. They passed a line out to the ship and used it as a lifeline to get to the ship. Rescuers went back and forth along the line ten times in storm tide seas in order to rescue the crew of the *E.S. Newman*.[6]

Michael A. Healy was born into slavery in 1840, the son of an African-American woman and a white man. At the age of fifteen, he ran away and was hired as a cabin boy aboard the clipper *Jumna*. He liked the life at sea and joined the Revenue Cutter Service in March 1865. He made his first cruise to Alaskan waters in 1868 as a young officer. From 1868 to 1895, Captain Michael A. Healy, an African American and runaway slave, sailed the waters of the Arctic Sea and

Alaska, commanding the cutters *Rush* and *Bear*. He was famous in his own day, the subject of several articles in the leading newspapers and magazines. Young boys all over America read about Healy and dreamed that they could grow up to have adventures like his. By 1881 he was a familiar figure from Attu to the Farallones Islands. Healy distinguished himself many times as an expert sailor and courageous lifesaver under the most extreme and demanding conditions.

In 1886 Healy became the captain of the cutter *Bear* when it first was put into service as a Revenue Service cutter. At that time, the seas around Alaska were crowded with whaling fleets, and prospectors poured into the country overland in their search for gold in the Klondike. Healy and his crew often risked their lives to rescue stranded prospectors and whalers or deliver

Captain Michael A. Healy

A native of Macon, Georgia, Michael A. Healy was the son of an Irish immigrant and a slave. In 1855, he ran away from home and signed on as a cabin boy aboard a clipper ship. In 1865, he applied to become a member of the Revenue Cutter Service. He started patrolling Alaskan waters in 1870. In 1884, he was the subject of a feature article in the New York *Sun*. His ship, the *Bear*, was considered by many the greatest polar ship of its time. Its responsibilities included catching sealers in the Bering Sea. He also brought medical supplies and other aid to people in Alaska, made weather and ice reports, prepared navigation charts, rescued vessels in distress, and transported special passengers.

medicine to remote settlements. When the *Bear* called at one of the stations up and down the coastline of Alaska, Captain Healy represented the authority of the United States government. He was responsible for saving lives, arresting lawbreakers, performing weddings, and delivering emergency medical supplies. Healy also made weather and ice reports, prepared navigational charts, rescued distressed vessels, and transported special passengers, such as the governor and important federal officials. Healy became a good friend to the local Inuits, or Eskimos.

The introduction of guns into the far Northwest had enabled the Inuits of northwestern Alaska to hunt the seals, walruses, and wild deer until the stocks became depleted. These native people lived almost entirely on meat. If the wild game that they hunted were to disappear, they would starve. On one of Healy's visits to King Island, he learned that the Inuit population was reduced to one hundred and the people were begging for food. Healy immediately ordered that they be given emergency food and clothing.

Healy convinced Dr. Sheldon Jackson of the Bureau of Education that the *Bear* should be used to bring reindeer to Alaska from Asia to begin a breeding herd that could be used to supply Alaskan Inuits with the means of survival. In 1891, Healy and Dr. Jackson cruised aboard the *Bear* to Seniavine Strait, Siberia, bought twelve reindeer, and took them back to Unalaska, Alaska. Over the next ten years, Revenue cutters brought more than eleven hundred reindeer to Alaska. By 1940, domestic reindeer herds in Alaska numbered over five hundred thousand animals. Over thirteen thousand Inuits lived by managing reindeer herds. Reindeer were used to feed their families, and they also sold reindeer and their products to consumers around the world.[7]

At the time of his retirement, Captain Healy was the third highest ranking officer in the Revenue Cutter Service. His contribution to the Coast Guard and in particular to the Alaskan territory was once highlighted in a New York *Sun* feature article that stated, "He stands for law and order in many thousand square miles of the land and water, and if you should ask in the Arctic Sea, 'Who is the greatest man in America?' the instant answer would be, 'Why, Mike Healy.'"[8]

After the Coast Guard Was Formed

During World War I, African Americans were permitted to serve in the Coast Guard only as messmen, working in ships' galleys, or kitchens. In World War II, however, President Franklin Delano Roosevelt decided the nation's military services should integrate. Following an announcement by the Secretary of Navy, Henry Knox, in April 1942, the Coast Guard admitted African Americans into regular service. One hundred fifty African Americans immediately volunteered and reported for training within a month. They slept and ate in segregated facilities, but they went through orientation and worked as radiomen, pharmacists, yeomen, coxswains, and electricians on shore as well as on buoy tenders and patrol boats. Many more African Americans entered the Coast Guard during World War II after the draft went into effect in December 1942. Most

The Coast Guard prides itself on its diversity. It welcomes anyone, regardless of race, ethnicity, or gender.

draftees were assigned shore duties at first, but the Coast Guard also integrated cutters in the summer of 1943. Since the end of the war, the Coast Guard has led the other services in the effort to achieve racial and gender equality in its ranks. Both African Americans and women are trained and expected to perform any

After four hard years, a young cadet holds her commission from the Coast Guard Academy on graduation day. In 1999, one-third of the student body at the Academy was female.

Alex Haley

Born in Ithaca, New York, August 11, 1921, Alex P. Haley graduated from high school at 15. He attended State Teacher's College in Elizabeth City, North Carolina, for two years and, at the urging of his father, enlisted in the Coast Guard in 1939 as a steward. Haley transferred to the journalist rate in 1949 and was the first Coast Guardsman to attain the rank of chief petty officer in that rate in 1950. His primary job was writing stories to promote the Coast Guard to the media. Haley later became a world-famous author and screenwriter. His best-known works include *Roots*, which received the 1977 Pulitzer Prize for fiction, and his collaboration on *The Autobiography of Malcolm X*.

duty the Coast Guard mission requires.

The Coast Guard has used the years of experience with female and African-American personnel to create a color- and sex-blind service prepared to meet the racial, ethnic, and cultural changes that affect America today. Applicants to the Coast Guard reflect this new America with its diversity and the challenges that such diversity presents.

The Future of the Coast Guard

The Department of Defense reports that in the immediate future, the major obstacles, or threats, to world peace will come from small-scale regional conflicts that can flare up at any time in any part of the world. The Coast Guard must be ready to assume more important defense and national security missions. Elements of the Defense Department's detection and monitoring tasks support maritime law enforcement. This will require additional Coast Guard maritime patrol aircraft and shipboard surveillance systems. The Coast Guard performs surveillance, intelligence, and patrol duties for military objectives under the Department of the Navy in such places as the Eastern Pacific Ocean and the Persian Gulf. The Coast Guard already oversees measures to protect the nation's marine environment and enforces laws against illegal immigration and the importation of illegal drugs on the seas. All of these activities require an enormous amount of money.

In 1999 the United States Congress voted $4.3 billion for the Coast Guard to continue to fulfill these responsibilities as well as its many other traditional tasks. This funding bill also ensured that while all current Coast Guard projects continue, outdated equipment would gradually be replaced with more modern versions, including new technology. The updating of equipment was needed to allow the Coast Guard to work hand in hand with the U.S. Navy to perform the new duties and joint operations that are envisioned by the Defense Department for the twenty-first century. This plan to gradually

The Coast Guard fights with the navy in wartime, and will need faster ships in the future. Cutters, such as the "Hamilton" class cutters, need to be updated to keep up with the United States Navy, Army, and Air Force.

723

U. S. COAST GUARD

723

replace outdated Coast Guard equipment is called "Deepwater."

To meet these new duty requirements, Coast Guard units must operate as a highly mobile quick-response force. Its ships and aircraft must match and work well with the U.S. Navy and Marine equipment that will be used in joint operations. At present, the Coast Guard uses three different types of cutters:

- The 378-foot "Hamilton" class

- The 270-foot "Reliance" class

- The 210-foot "Reliance" class

All these cutters are quickly becoming hard to maintain and technologically outdated. They also require a crew of 20 officers and 150 enlisted personnel. A new "Deepwater" system of cutters will

Ships like this 270-foot "Reliance" cutter can carry up to 20 officers and 150 crewmen. In the future new cutters will be made that are smaller and faster.

COAST GUARD   904

require smaller crews of only ninety people. The cutters will be faster, better equipped, and able to patrol for longer periods of time. Coast Guard aircraft face the same general problems as the cutters. A new helicopter that can operate with the swifter new cutters is needed. The Coast Guard is considering the HV-609, an experimental tilt-wing craft that takes off like a helicopter but flies like a fixed-wing plane, reaching speeds of over 275 miles per hour with a range of 750 miles or more. The present Coast Guard fixed-wing aircraft are being upgraded with Global Positioning System receivers and better radar and other surveillance equipment.[1]

Along with the new cutters and aircraft, a new generation of intelligence and information-gathering systems is also being put into operation. Satellites and sensors will provide real-time information allowing total visibility in U.S. territorial waters and beyond. This sort of instant visibility increases the likelihood of both intercepting and stopping drug boats and pinpointing the precise location of wrecks and other disasters. The Coast Guard is also updating vessel and harbor communications networks and command centers. All of this will contribute to a world-class waterways management system under Coast Guard leadership.

During the 1990s the number of Coast Guard personnel fell to its lowest point since 1967. The Coast Guard is trying to downsize its overall personnel requirements as it upgrades to better equipment that requires fewer people to run it. However, in 1998 the Coast Guard was forced to operate with more than 1,000 of its 28,126 positions left unfilled. The 1999 funding bill authorized the Coast Guard to fill those positions and remain at full strength.

In order to meet its personnel needs, the Coast Guard wants to attract young people who are motivated and willing to learn and who have varied interests and skills. There is a great need for electronics technicians and mechanics for all the different types of Coast Guard boats and aircraft. Recruits with only basic knowledge will be given training for such work. Bilingual or multilingual personnel, who speak English

Aircraft are crucial during search-and-rescue operations. In fact, HH-65 Dolphins have rescued more people worldwide than any other type of helicopter.

and any other languages, including Inuit and other Eskimo dialects, Spanish, French, and Chinese, are in great demand. Coast Guard personnel with college degrees in business are needed to administer bridges and harbors. It will be the Coast Guard's men and women—shaped by professionalism, leadership, and selfless humanitarian service—who will continue to uphold the Coast Guard tradition of service to the country and its citizens.[2]

Coast Guard Equipment

HH-60J "Jayhawk" Medium-Range Recovery Helicopter

The HH-60J "Jayhawk" is a medium-range recovery helicopter. It is 65 feet long and has an empty weight of 14,500 pounds. In addition, the helicopter carries 6,460 pounds of fuel. It is powered by two General Electric T700-401C gas turbine engines and can reach speeds of over 200 miles per hour. It has a maximum range of over 800 miles. It is operated by two pilots

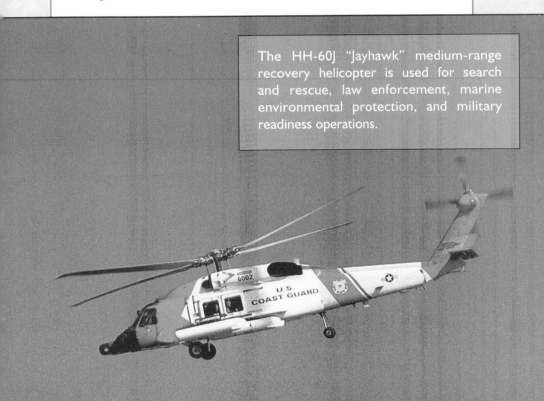

The HH-60J "Jayhawk" medium-range recovery helicopter is used for search and rescue, law enforcement, marine environmental protection, and military readiness operations.

and two crewmen. The HH-60J is used to perform search and rescue, law enforcement, marine environmental protection, and military readiness missions. The HH-60J is usually stationed ashore, but it can land and take off from both 270-foot and 378-foot Coast Guard cutters. These cutters carry both fuel and maintenance crews for the "Jayhawk" helicopter.

HC-130 "Hercules" Long-Range Surveillance Aircraft

The HC-130 "Hercules" is a long-range surveillance and transport fixed-wing airplane. It is slightly over 97 feet long, has a wingspan of 132 feet, and has an empty weight of 76,780 pounds. It can carry 62,900

The HC-130 "Hercules," known as the "Herky," is a long-range surveillance and transport airplane capable of carrying more than ninety people. The Coast Guard uses it for law enforcement and search and rescue missions.

pounds of fuel. It is powered by four Allison T56-A15 turboprop engines. The "Hercules" operates with two pilots and a crew of five. It can cruise at over 300 miles per hour and has a maximum range of over 4,500 miles. It is a general-purpose aircraft for the Coast Guard and is used to perform search and rescue, illegal drug interdiction, marine environmental protection, and ice patrol missions as well as cargo and personnel transport.

HH-65A "Dolphin" Short-Range Recovery Helicopter

The HH-65A "Dolphin" is a short-range recovery helicopter. It is slightly over 44 feet long and has an empty weight of 6,092 pounds. It can carry up to 1,900 pounds of fuel to run two Lycoming LTS-101-750B-2 gas turbine engines. It can cruise at over 120 miles per hour and has a maximum range of over 300 miles. It is operated by two pilots and a crew of two. It is used for search and rescue; enforcement of laws and treaties, including drug interdiction; polar patrol; marine environmental protection, including pollution control; and military readiness missions. Like the larger HH-60J "Jayhawk," the HH-65A is usually based ashore. However, the HH-65A can land and take off from 210-foot, 270-foot, and 378-foot Coast Guard cutters. These cutters are capable of refueling and supporting the helicopter for the duration of a cutter patrol.

RU-38A Surveillance Aircraft

The RU-38A covert surveillance aircraft is especially designed to conduct both low-level and high-altitude observation and tracking missions for the Coast Guard. It is powered by two turbocharged engines in a "push-pull" design, with one engine in front and one engine at the back of the cabin. It can safely operate on one of the engines to increase its range and time aloft. The RU-38A makes little noise and gives off only a small amount of heat in order to avoid detection at low altitudes. It is specially designed to carry various kinds of multi-sensor payloads that can be placed on the plane on pallets so that the plane can quickly change from low- to high-altitude missions.

USCG *Dauntless* (WMEC-624)

Like all ships in the "Reliance" class of 210-foot medium-endurance cutters, *Dauntless* is named for an aspirational trait, in this case meaning "fearlessly persevering." Its home port is Galveston, Texas. *Dauntless* was commissioned in 1967. It served in the Vietnam War. In 1986, it was the first cutter to arrive at the scene of the space shuttle *Challenger* disaster. In 1993, it underwent a complete overhaul, which cost $21 million. Two years later it rescued 578 immigrants from a coastal freighter in trouble. Today the *Dauntless* is a "drug buster." As of 1999, its crew had seized more than one million pounds of marijuana in more than eighty-five narcotics "busts."

NAVTEX Early Warning System

NAVTEX is an international automated system for instantly distributing maritime navigational warnings, weather forecasts, and search and rescue notices to ships. When a ship first enters one of the designated areas, all of the previous messages that are of interest to the ship will be sent and received on a self-contained "smart" radio receiver that prints the messages on a roll of paper. No one needs to be present during a broadcast to receive this vital information. New messages will automatically be received and printed as long as the ship remains in that area.

COSPAS-Search and Rescue Satellite

The COSPAS-SARSAT is a part of the Global Maritime Distress and Safety System, an international satellite-based search and rescue system established by Canada, France, Russia, and the United States. These four countries jointly helped develop a 406-Megahertz satellite emergency position-indicating radio beacon that is activated by a special radio onboard a ship at sea in distress. This automatic distress-call transmitter, which is now required on most oceangoing commercial ships and fishing vessels, will send the distressed ship's identification and exact position to a rescue coordination center from anywhere in the world.

HU-25A "Guardian" Medium-Range Surveillance Jet

The HU-25A "Guardian" is a medium-range, all-weather surveillance and search and rescue aircraft. It is slightly longer than 56 feet and has a wingspan of more than 53 feet. It is powered by two Garrett ATF3-6A-4C jet engines. It weighs 18,188 pounds empty and carries 10,681 pounds of fuel. It can cruise at 30,000 feet at a speed of 541 miles per hour. It has a range of nearly 3,000 miles with eight passengers. It has a normal crew of two pilots, two observers, and a sensor systems operator. The plane is normally equipped with AN/APS-127 radar and state-of-the-art communications equipment. The "Guardian" has also been fitted with two observation windows and a drop

The HU-25A "Guardian" is a medium-range jet used for surveillance and search and rescue missions. It can carry eight passengers and has a range of 3,000 miles.

hatch for rescue supplies, which typically weigh up to 3,200 pounds.

USCG *Eagle* (WIX-327)

The *Eagle* is a three-masted sailing ship that carries 21,350 square feet of sail. It is 295 feet long and has a maximum speed of 11 to 16 knots under full sail. Its hull and decks are constructed of steel four-tenths of an inch thick. The decks are covered with teakwood. The *Eagle* carries a crew of twelve officers and thirty-eight crewmen. It is the only active commissioned sailing ship in the United States maritime service. It was constructed in 1936 in Hamburg, Germany, and taken as a prize during World War II. It is homeported at the Coast Guard Academy in New London, Connecticut. It serves as a training vessel for Academy cadets. Each cruise, 150 cadets work as deckhands, learning the names of the sails and more than 200 different lines used to control them as well as navigation and other skills.

USCGC *Healy* (WAGB 20)

The *Healy* is the world's largest non–nuclear-powered icebreaker. It was designed both as an icebreaker to aid navigation and as a research vessel for polar scientific missions. It is 420 feet long and displaces over 16,000 tons of water. The ship is propelled by diesel-powered electric engines that develop over 16,000 horsepower. The ship's engines are located on the main deck in order to reduce the noise for the sonar equipment located in the hull. The ship has a crew of seventy-five and has room for up to eighty-five scientists. The *Healy* can cruise at about 15 miles per hour and has a range of 30,000 nautical miles. It carries over a million gallons of fuel. The ship carries modern sonar and satellite communications equipment. The *Healy* is designed to operate over two hundred days a year and is capable of wintering over on the ice.

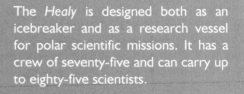

The *Healy* is designed both as an icebreaker and as a research vessel for polar scientific missions. It has a crew of seventy-five and can carry up to eighty-five scientists.

Chapter Notes

Chapter 1. Extraordinary Lifesavers

1. Leslie Hazelton, "Surf Wars," *Boating*, vol. 70, no. 3, March 1997, pp. 126–132.

Chapter 2. History of the Coast Guard

1. Anthony Wilson, *Visual Timeline of Transportation* (New York: Dorling Kindersley, 1995), p. 14.

2. "Year of the Ocean," *National Oceanic and Atmospheric Administration Page*, n.d., <http://www.yoto98.noaa.gov/yoto/meeting/nat_sec-316.html> (June 1, 2000).

3. "African Americans in the Coast Guard," *United States Coast Guard Page*, n.d., <http://www.uscg.mil/hq/g-cp/history/h_Africanamericans.html> (January 9, 2001).

4. Truman R. Strobridge and Dennis L. Noble, *Alaska and the U.S. Revenue Cutter Service 1867–1915* (Annapolis, Md.: Naval Institute Press, 1999), pp. 67–68.

5. Ibid., p. 5.

6. Van Field, "Additional Notes: The United States Life-Saving Service," *Long Island Genealogy Page*, n.d., <http://www.longislandgenealogy.com/lifesaving.html> (March 23, 2001).

7. Dennis L. Noble, *That Others Might Live: The U.S. Life-Saving Service, 1878–1915* (Annapolis, Md.: Naval Institute Press, 1994), p. 59.

8. Wilson, p. 24.

9. Noble, p. 77.

10. Malcolm F. Willoughby, *The U.S. Coast Guard in World War II* (Annapolis, Md.: Naval Institute Press, 1957), pp. 98, 197.

11. "Frequently Asked Questions About Recruiting," *United States Coast Guard Page*, January 8, 2001, <http://www.uscg.mil/hq/recruit/faq.htm #where> (January 9, 2001).

Chapter 3. People of the Coast Guard

1. "Atlantic Area Overview," *United States Coast Guard Page*, January 2000, <http://uscg.mil/lantarea/ Overview/overview.html> (June 1, 2000).

2. "Coast Guard Enlistment," *Military Career Guide Online*, n.d., <http://www.militarycareers. com/OCC/coaenlst.html> (November 19, 2000).

3. U.S. Department of Labor, Bureau of Labor Statistics, *1998–1999 Occupational Outlook Handbook* (Washington, D.C.: Department of Labor, 1999), p. 1318.

4. "U.S. Coast Guard Officer Candidate School," *United States Coast Guard Page*, January 8, 2000, <http://www.uscg.mil/hq/uscga/ldc/ocs/index.htm> (June 3, 2000).

5. "Female Cadets Gaining Sway at the Coast Guard Academy," *The New York Times*, November 15, 1999, section B, p. 6.

6. "U.S. Coast Guard Academy Review," *United States Coast Guard Page*, November 2000, <http://www.cga.edu/admiss/overview.html> (June 3, 2000).

7. Howard B. Thorsen, "The Coast Guard in Review," *Proceedings of the United States Naval Institute*, vol. 125, no. 5, May 1999, pp. 94–98.

Chapter 4. Structure of the Coast Guard

1. "Our History," *United States Coast Guard Page*, n.d., <http://www.uscg.mil> (March 21, 2001).

2. "Organizational Chart," *United States Coast Guard Page*, January 2001, <http://www.uscg.mil/images/graphics/org.html> (March 21, 2001).

3. "Operating Expenses Budget by Major Programs—Fiscal Year 2001," *United States Coast Guard Page*, n.d., <http://www.uscg.mil/news/bib/BIBprint.pdf> (March 21, 2001).

Chapter 5. Duties of the Coast Guard

1. Jerry Kirschenbaum and Brayton Harris, *Safe Boat: A Comprehensive Guide to the Purchase, Equipping, Maintenance, and Operation of a Safe Boat* (New York: W.W. Norton & Company, 1990), p. 9.

2. Howard B. Thorsen, "The Coast Guard in Review," *Proceedings of the United States Naval Institute*, vol. 125, no. 5, May, 1999, pp. 94–98.

3. Kirschenbaum and Harris, p. 144.

4. Ibid., p. 188.

5. Ibid., p. 204.

6. "417 U.S. Bound Haitians Forced to Return Home," *Jet*, vol. 93, no. 5, December 22, 1997, p. 11.

7. "Year of the Ocean," *National Oceanic and Atmospheric Administration Page*, n.d., <http://www.yoto98.noaa.gov/yoto/meeting/nat_sec-316.html> (June 1, 2000).

8. Thorsen, pp. 94–98.

9. "Year of the Ocean."

Chapter 6. Women and Minorities in the Coast Guard

1. Elizabeth A. Neely, "A Thumbnail History of Women in the Coast Guard," *Jack's Joint Page*, n.d., <http://www.jacksjoint.com/cgwomen.htm> (June 1, 2000).

2. "What was a SPAR?" *Lighthouse Digest Magazine*, September 1999, <http://www.lhdigest.com/archives/1999/September_1999/spar.html> (June 1, 2000).

3. Ibid.

4. Neely.

5. "African Americans in the Coast Guard," *United States Coast Guard Page*, January 1999, <http://www.uscg.mil/hq/g-cp/history/h_Africanamericans.html> (June 1, 2000).

6. Ibid.

7. Truman R. Strobridge and Dennis L. Noble, *Alaska and the U.S. Revenue Cutter Service 1867–1915* (Annapolis, Md.: Naval Institute Press, 1999), p. 148ff.

8. Stephen H. Evans, *The United States Coast Guard 1798–1915* (Annapolis, Md.: Naval Institute Press, 1968), p. 121.

Chapter 7. The Future of the Coast Guard

1. Ernest Blazer, "Moving into the Next Century," *Sea Power*, vol. 42, no. 8, August 1999, p. 339.

2. "Coast Guard Receives $4.3 Billion for FY," *Sea Power*, vol. 41, no. 12, December 1998, p. 21.

Glossary

below—Anywhere beneath the main deck of a ship.

bow—The front end of a ship.

cutter—A ship of 65 feet or more in length that will accommodate a crew for long cruises. They were the first Coast Guard ships, and today the Coast Guard still calls its ships "cutters."

icebreakers—Slow-moving ships with reinforced bottoms designed to move onto the ice and break it with their great weight. Icebreakers too can become frozen into the ice.

Life-Saving Service—Founded in 1848, the Life-Saving Service maintained rescue equipment and saved thousands of lives during its existence. The Life-Saving Service was merged with the Revenue Service in 1915 to form the United States Coast Guard.

lighthouse—A structure that shines a warning light to alert boats of all sizes of nearby dangers and to help pilots navigate their ships safely through nearby water.

Lighthouse Service—Founded in 1789, the Lighthouse Service maintained the lighthouses and other navigational aids along U.S. coastal and inland waterways until it was merged with the U.S. Coast Guard in 1939.

main deck—The uppermost deck of a ship that extends from bow to stern (front to back).

port—The left-hand side of a ship when one is standing on deck facing the bow (front).

quarterdeck—On sailing ships, the deck above the main deck that extends from the stern a quarter of the way to the bow.

Revenue Service—Founded in 1789, the Revenue Service became the backbone of the modern U.S. Coast Guard. The merger of the Revenue Service and the Life-Saving Service formed the U.S. Coast Guard in 1915.

rigging—On a sailing ship, the ropes, chains, and other gear that support the masts and work the sails used to move a ship through the water.

starboard—The right-hand side of a ship when one is standing on deck facing the bow (front).

stern—The back end of a ship.

Further Reading

Anderson, Madelyn. *Sea Raids and Rescues: The United States Coast Guard*. New York: McKay, 1979.

Ferrel, Nancy Warren. *The United States Coast Guard*. Minneapolis: Lerner Publishing, 1989.

Hale, Dorothy. *The Coast Guard and You*. New York: Maxwell Macmillan International, 1993.

Naden, Corinne and Rose Blue. *The United States Coast Guard*. Brookfield, Conn.: Millbrook, 1993.

Stefoff, Rebecca. *The United States Coast Guard*. New York: Chelsea House, 1989.

Van Orden, M.D. *U.S. Navy Ships and Coast Guard Cutters*. Annapolis, Md.: Naval Institute Press, 1990.

Internet Addresses

U.S. Coast Guard Web site
<http://www.uscg.mil>

U.S. Coast Guard Academy Web site
<http://www.cga.edu>

U.S. Coast Guard Navigation Center Web site
<http://www.navcen.uscg.gov>

Index